Monetarism

Monetarism
THEORY, EVIDENCE & POLICY

Howard R. Vane & John L. Thompson
Liverpool Polytechnic

A HALSTED PRESS BOOK

John Wiley & Sons
NEW YORK

First published in the U.K. 1979 by Martin Robertson & Company Ltd., 108 Cowley Road, Oxford OX4 1JF. Published in the U.S.A. 1979 by Halsted Press, a Division of John Wiley & Sons, Inc., New York.

Library of Congress Cataloging in Publication Data

Vane, Howard R.
   Monetarism, theory, evidence & policy.

   "A Halsted Press book."
   Includes index.
   1. Money, 2. Monetary policy.   I. Thompson, John L.,
joint author.   II. Title.
HG221.V34   1979   332.4   78-24173
ISBN 0-470-26569-8

Typeset by Preface Ltd., Salisbury.
Printed and bound in the U.K. by Richard Clay Ltd.,
at The Chaucer Press, Bungay, Suffolk.

Contents

Preface

In recent years the question of the importance of money in macro-economic theory has been the subject of considerable controversy. Traditional theory developed during the 1950s and 1960s tended to regard money as having only limited importance with respect to the determination of macroeconomic variables. In contrast to this belief, an alternative view was developed during the 1960s stressing the importance of the quantity of money. Economists who subscribe to this belief are called monetarists, and the use of this term indicates the emphasis they place on the role of the quantity of money in the determination of national income. This book is directed towards an examination of the issues involved in this dispute.

Although monetarism is one of the central issues debated within macroeconomics today, there is a gap in the literature presenting the overall framework of monetarism in a form suitable for students in the second or third year of an undergraduate course. All too often standard undergraduate texts include only a brief summary of the issues involved. The main aim of the text is to fill this gap and provide an account of the theoretical and empirical foundations on which monetarism is based. This will, of course, automatically entail an examination of the policy prescriptions of monetarism. As this book is primarily intended for students taking a macroeconomics course in either the second or third year of their degree, we have presumed that such students will have a firm grasp of both basic economic principles and also be familiar with the *IS–LM* model. Therefore, no attempt has been made to explain the derivation and manipulation of the *IS–LM* model for the closed economy. Wherever possible a verbal and geometric presentation has been used. In the instances where an algebraic presentation is essential, this analysis has been generally relegated to appendices. The book should also be useful to undergraduate students taking courses in monetary and international economics and to postgraduate students in their preliminary year of study.

Many people have helped us in the preparation of this book, to all of whom we would like to express our gratitude. We are especially indebted to Richard Harrington (Manchester University) who read the draft chapters and made many helpful suggestions and comments. We would also like to thank David Peel (Liverpool University) and Alasdair Lonie (Dundee University) for helpful suggestions. We are grateful to Christine and Margaret for their help in preparing and checking the draft manuscript. Our final thanks go to the ladies in the typing pool, in particular Sheila Bruce, Joyce Parker and Margaret Woods, for their patience and cooperation in the typing of the final manuscript. Any remaining errors are our responsibility.

H. R. Vane *(Department of Social Studies)*

April, 1978 J. L. Thompson *(Department of Business Studies)*

To Christine and Margaret

1 The Basic Theoretical Propositions of Monetarism

1.1 Introduction

'The central issue that is debated these days in connection with macroeconomics is the doctrine of monetarism' (Samuelson, 1969). This comment is as relevant today as when it was made nearly a decade ago. Monetarism is concerned with the role of money in macroeconomic theory and with the operation of short-run stabilisation policy. In essence, monetarists emphasise the potency of money and stress the importance of following a monetary rule in the conduct of monetary policy in order to avoid economic instability. The central importance attached to the conduct of monetary policy, although still a controversial issue today, contrasts sharply with the general stance taken in the period from the 1930s through to the 1950s.

In the 1930s the central problem facing economists was the need to provide an explanation of, and remedy for, the then-prevailing severe unemployment. Keynes (1936) put forward the view that the Great Depression (1929–33 for the United States) was the result of a sharp fall in the level of investment, and that unemployment reflected a state of deficient aggregate demand. A major theme, interpreted from the General Theory by Keynes's disciples and by policy-makers, was that monetary policy would be ineffective in preventing the substantial unemployment which was regarded as the normal state of an advanced capitalist economy. Instead, the importance of fiscal policy (via government spending and/or tax cuts) was stressed to prevent the economy from settling at a position of underemployment equilibrium. Since government expenditure is

3

a component of aggregate demand, Keynesians believed that an increase in government expenditure would have a strong and direct effect in reducing the level of unemployment. In contrast, changes in the money supply were held to operate indirectly through changes in the rate of interest which would alter private investment. As interest rates were low during this period, the depression was interpreted by Keynesians as demonstrating the inadequacy of monetary policy. These beliefs became embodied within standard undergraduate textbooks which belittled the role of monetary policy and stressed the importance of fiscal policy as the main tool of macroeconomic policy. It should be noted that, according to Leijonhufvud's (1968) reinterpretation, Keynes himself strongly believed in the power of monetary policy to stabilise the economy, except perhaps in conditions of deep depression. Here fiscal pump-priming might be used to revive expectations regarding profitable investment opportunities.

After the Second World War it was widely feared that, owing to a lack of investment opportunities, a period of depression would ensue. In order to avoid heavy unemployment, it was argued that expansionary policy measures (especially fiscal measures) would be required to stimulate investment and consumption. In the years immediately following the war it was generally agreed that money did not matter very much for analysing aggregate demand and unemployment; and therefore no real attempt was made to control the money supply. A policy of keeping interest rates low was followed in order to keep down the interest cost of government debt and also to allow for the possibility of providing some stimulus to investment, although it was thought that investment was not particularly sensitive to the rate of interest.

The revival in the belief in the potency of monetary policy in the United States was associated with the so-called monetarist counter-revolution. A major initiating force in this revival came from the work of the Chicago School under the leadership of Milton Friedman. Re-examining the monetary history of the period of the Great Depression, they have argued that the depression was a consequence of monetary change (between October 1929 and June 1933, the US money stock fell by about a third), and that the trough in economic activity that followed was prolonged owing to the lack of a sufficiently expansionary monetary policy. Friedman and his associates have interpreted the depression as demonstrating the potency, rather than the ineffectiveness, of monetary policy. They have further argued that the inflation of the postwar years was stimulated by the widespread adoption of cheap-money policies and has, therefore, been the automatic consequence of excessive money creation. As a result, the Chicago School have prescribed control of the money supply as being essential to avoid the instability of either depression or inflation. By the end of the 1960s the controversy in the United States over the potency of money and the role of monetary policy crystalised into the so-called monetarist–fiscalist debate. This ongoing debate has involved an evaluation of monetary versus fiscal policy, in which monetarism has come to be associated with rules and guidelines and fiscalism with activism and discretion.

In this opening chapter we shall outline the major theoretical propositions characterising the monetarist viewpoint as these form part of the foundation on which monetarist policy prescriptions are based. This will provide an introductory framework to the essentially theoretical analyses of chapters 2, 3 and 4 before we examine monetarist views on the conduct and role of monetary and fiscal policy in chapters 5 and 6 respectively. We would like to stress that, for the sake of ease of exposition, in this and subsequent chapters we refer to Keynesians and monetarists as if they were two opposed, unified and consistent schools of thought. However, the reader should bear in mind that this simplification has been adopted purely for analytical convenience. In practice there is a considerable degree of overlap between the two schools so that an economist can lean towards monetarism for certain matters and towards a Keynesian viewpoint for others. Also, for many issues an intermediate or eclectic position is both possible and respectable.

Within the school of economists referred to as monetarists there are differences of opinion and emphasis, and it is therefore impossible to produce a definitive list of characteristics of the monetarist viewpoint which would be universally acceptable. We shall therefore begin by outlining the major theoretical propositions that provide the basic tenor of monetarist views. These propositions are centred on a belief in the dominance and nature of monetary impulses; a distinct version of the transmission mechanism whereby monetary influences affect spending decisions generally; a belief in the inherent stability of the private sector; and the view that allocative detail is largely irrelevant to the explanation of short-run changes in nominal income.

1.2   The Dominance of Monetary Impulses

1.2.1   *The quantity theory: old and new*

Within monetarist analysis, monetary forces are assigned a dominant position in determining the course of economic activity. It is argued that changes in the money stock are the predominant, though not the only, factor explaining changes in nominal income (real income is regarded as being determined by real factors). This belief is embodied within the quantity theory of money which goes back to before the seventeenth century.

The quantity theory of money may be formulated and analysed in terms of the relationship:

$$MV = PO \qquad\qquad (1.1)$$

where M refers to the nominal money supply; V refers to the income velocity of circulation of money (or the inverse of the real quantity of money demanded per unit of output – see appendix 1 to this chapter), and PO refers to the money value of output produced and is referred to henceforth simply as nominal income.

Within this relationship changes in nominal income can be produced by either changes in the nominal money balances *(M)* available for people to hold (the supply of money), or by changes in the real balances that people wish to hold (i.e. the demand for money, thus causing changes in V). If the demand for money is unstable, unpredictable changes in V are likely to occur so that knowledge that the supply of money had increased would not allow a precise prediction of how much, if at all, nominal income would increase. This is the position adopted in the Radcliffe Report (1959), and the flavour of their views can be gauged from the following extract: 'we cannot find any reason for supposing, or any experience in monetary history, indicating that there is any limit to the velocity of circulation . . . .' (para. 391).

In its traditional form the quantity theory refers to a body of doctrine concerned with the relationship between the money supply and the general price level. The classical quantity theory held that the general price level (P) was determined solely by the money supply (M). Any change in the money supply would lead to a proportionate change in the general price level, since velocity was taken to be numerically stable (i.e. constant) in the short run and output was held to tend always towards a position of full employment, which was itself determined by real factors.

In contrast, within Friedman's restatement (1956) the quantity theory is taken in the first instance to be a theory of the demand for money, rather than a theory of the price level or nominal income. In practice however, the additional assumptions necessary to make predictions about nominal income are invariably made in the modern quantity theory. Monetarists contend that there exists a stable functional relationship between the demand for real balances and a limited number of variables, but it is behaviour that is held to be stable so that velocity is not regarded as being a numerical constant over time. Moreover, they argue that empirical evidence has shown that changes in desired real balances tend to proceed slowly and gradually, or are the result of events set in motion by prior changes in the supply of money. On the other hand, it is held that substantial changes in the supply of nominal balances can and frequently have occurred independently of any changes in the demand for money. In terms of the quantity theory relationship (equation 1.1), movements in velocity are believed to be minor relative to changes in the supply of money and are taken to reinforce rather than offset movements in the money supply. Monetarists then do not claim that velocity is constant but that it is sufficiently stable to provide a predictable relationship between changes in the money supply and changes in nominal income (see chapter 2 for a detailed discussion of the demand for money function). With present knowledge and techniques they also argue that any attempt to offset any minor changes that could occur in V by a discretionary monetary policy is likely to make matters worse rather than better. To summarise this argument then, monetarists contend that, in the face of a stable demand for money, most of the observed instability in the economy is attributable to fluctuations in the money supply induced by the monetary authorities.

1.2.2 *Endogeneity of the money supply*

One of the major criticisms levied against this monetarist view is that under certain circumstances the money supply will become endogenous and that as a result causation will run from income to money (rather than vice versa) and hence inferences drawn from regressions of income on money are worthless. Monetarists accept that under certain circumstances the money supply will become endogenous but contend that recognition of this does not imply the abandonment of the causal role attributed to money. (The money supply process is examined in detail in chapter 3.) They argue that the authorities can control the money supply if they choose to do so and that if the money supply is controlled then the path that nominal income will follow will be different from a situation where the money supply is endogenous. Monetarists also argue that, given the relative stability of velocity, the use of the money supply as a policy instrument would permit the control of the level of economic activity.

1.2.3   *Monetary impulses: three important distinctions*

Having outlined the belief that changes in the money stock are the predominant factor explaining changes in nominal income, it is important to note three crucial distinctions in discussing monetary impulses. These distinctions relate to the different roles attributed to monetary acceleration (or deceleration) and monetary growth, the impact of monetary factors on real and nominal variables, and the distinction between short- and long-run effects.

The basic source of short-run economic instability is held to be monetary actions which result in accelerations or decelerations in the rate of growth of the money supply. Before one can say whether, for example, a 15 per cent annual rate of increase of the money stock would cause an expansion or contraction of nominal income, it is necessary to know what the previous rate of monetary growth was. If the rate of monetary growth was 10 per cent in the previous years, then increasing this rate to 15 per cent would have an expansionary effect. If, on the other hand, the previous monetary growth rate was 20 per cent, then a reduction to 15 per cent would have a contractionary effect on nominal income. Monetarist analysis suggests that in order to predict the effect on nominal income of monetary policy changes, it is essential to determine whether these result in an acceleration or deceleration in the rate of monetary growth.

In the short run, monetary changes are viewed as operating mainly on output and employment, but after a time lag it is believed that prices will rise and that the long-run effect will be mainly on prices. The impact of monetary accelerations (or decelerations) on output and employment is then viewed as being essentially temporary, with the timing and strength of the impact depending upon the initial conditions at the time of a change in the rate of monetary growth. In the long run, it is argued that the trend rate of monetary growth influences movements in the price level and other nominal variables. The trend movement in real variables (e.g. output and employment) is believed to be essentially determined independently of monetary forces by the growth of real factors, such as the labour force, capital stock and the state of technology. (See chapter 4 for a discussion of money and inflation.)

1.2.4 *The Keynesian view*

The modern quantity theory belief that changes in the money stock are the predominant factor explaining changes in nominal income is one of the key propositions that differentiate monetarists from Keynesians. As with the monetarist viewpoint, it is extremely difficult to produce a definitive list of characteristics that would be accepted by all Keynesians alike. This problem is magnified by Leijonhufvud's work (1968, 1969), which has drawn a sharp distinction between the economics of Keynes and Keynesian economics. Indeed, it has been suggested that Keynes, in contrast to conventional Keynesian doctrine, attributed an important role to money and monetary policy in controlling the economy. Keynesian analysis, however, in interpreting changes in nominal income, has traditionally emphasised the relationship between nominal income and investment or autonomous expenditure. Although it is not claimed that changes in the money stock are unimportant, modern Keynesian analysis, in contrast to monetarism, denies that changes in the money stock dominate changes in nominal income, except perhaps in the long run.

In terms of the quantity theory of money the message taken from Keynes's (1936) General Theory was that in conditions of under-employment (which it was held could prevail for long periods of time) velocity would be highly unstable and would passively adapt to whatever changes occurred independently in nominal income or the money stock. Under such conditions then, although the quantity equation would be entirely valid, Keynesians argued that it would be largely useless for policy or prediction, especially in the short run.

Nowadays, while modern Keynesians no longer seem to believe that the demand for money is highly unstable, they do however take the possibility of an unstable demand for money function more seriously than do monetarists. The question of how stable is stable is still raised, and Radcliffians would still deny, for example, that the UK demand for money is stable enough to permit great reliance on monetary policy. Doubts are raised over the existence of a stable demand for money function owing to a belief that the statistical evidence derived from periods of endogenous money is irrelevant for predictions in periods when the money supply is controlled and a belief that the margin between money and near money is a shifting one.

1.2.5   *The quantity theory in an open economy*

The quantity theory of money has been discussed so far only within the context of a closed economy. By extending the analysis to an international setting, the basic quantity theory proposition is broadened to embrace the view that, in a world of fixed exchange rates, inflation is an international monetary phenomenon. (The international aspects of inflation are examined more fully in chapter 4.) In an open economy, with fixed exchange rates, monetarists argue that nations are linked together into a world economy in which the aggregate world money supply (the sum of the individual nation's money supplies) determines world prices. Therefore in this case, in contrast to a closed economy, where domestic monetary expansion relative to the growth of real output determines the domestic rate of inflation, domestic monetary expansion or contraction will influence the domestic rate of inflation only to the extent that it influences the rate of change of the world money supply and, in consequence, the rate of change of world prices.

Implicit in this viewpoint is the belief that the balance of payments is a monetary phenomenon and requires the application of monetary theory to its understanding. This belief also forms a central part of the analysis of the international transmission of inflation in a world of fixed exchange rates. The monetary approach to balance of payments theory, as with the quantity theory, focuses primarily on the money market and the relationship between the demand for and supply of money. The monetary approach postulates a direct relationship between the money supply and the balance of payments.

Under flexible exchange rates, however, the relationship between the demand for and supply of money is held to determine the exchange rate. The rate of domestic inflation will be determined by domestic monetary policy and any difference between the domestic and the rest of the world's inflation rates will cause the exchange rate to adjust. (The monetary approach to the balance of payments is discussed in detail in chapter 7.)

1.3 The transmission mechanism

1.3.1 *The monetarist transmission mechanism*

The focus assigned to the nominal money supply, and the demand for real money balances in monetarist thinking, leads to another associated proposition of monetarism, that of a distinct version of the transmission mechanism whereby monetary influences affect spending decisions through a portfolio adjustment process. It is argued that, when actual money balances are out of line with desired money balances (owing for example to an increase in the money supply), stocks of both financial and non-financial assets are altered in order to restore equilibrium between desired and actual money balances. Within this approach money is regarded as a substitute for all assets alike, real and financial, rather than as a close substitute for only a small range of financial assets. Any discrepancy between actual and desired money balances may be eliminated by spending on a wide range of goods and services. It may affect not only expenditure on financial assets but also expenditure on non-durable and durable goods, investment in education, and investment in durable producers' goods. (For a fuller discussion of the portfolio adjustment process and the monetarist transmission mechanism see chapter 2.)

1.3.2 *The Keynesian transmission mechanism*

In contrast, within the Keynesian analysis of the transmission mechanism the effect of changes in the money supply on expenditure takes place almost entirely by way of changes in interest rates on financial assets. In response, for example, to an excess supply of money, short-term liquid (i.e. those that are easily convertible into money) assets will be purchased and this will cause their price to rise and their yield to decrease. This will, in turn, lead to purchases of less liquid financial assets along the liquidity spectrum and eventually will cause a change in yields at the long end of the financial market. The resulting divergence between the cost of capital and the return on capital will lead to an increase in investment spending and therefore to an increase in income.

By adopting a borrowing cost interpretation, the Keynesian transmission mechanism typically treats an increase in the money supply as affecting only investment and not consumption. Interest rates are lowered by an increase in the money stock and, owing to the lower borrowing cost, demand is stimulated for goods bought with credit. It is further held that the transmission of monetary impulses depends on the response of a small proportion of expenditure categories with comparatively high borrowing costs. Expenditure on business investment, residential construction and central and local authority construction may be stimulated owing to the cost of credit channel. Investment in consumer durables (often bought with credit) may also be increased, but the demand for non-durable goods will not be directly affected as these are not usually bought on credit. Increased investment spending will in turn affect total spending via the multiplier.

1.3.3   The distinction between the Keynesian and monetarist transmission mechanisms

It can be argued that the difference between Keynesians and monetarists lies in the range of assets considered, rather than in the nature of the process. The crucial distinction involves the different viewpoints as to the degree to which certain assets may be regarded as close substitutes for money. Keynesians view financial assets as close substitutes for money, whereas monetarists regard money as a substitute for all assets alike, real or financial, and stress a much broader and more direct impact on spending.

This difference in the range of assets considered is illustrated by the different view as to the price of money. The Keynesian approach tends to regard the interest rate as the price of money since money can be lent or held, whereas quantity theorists take the inverse of the price level as the price of money, with the interest rate being viewed as the price of credit. This is partly due to the way in which Keynesian portfolio balance theory was developed with the assumption of an actual or expected stable price level, while the restated quantity theory introduced changes in the price level as a factor affecting the demand for money.

1.3.4 *The transmission mechanism: additional comments*

It is possible to accept the Keynesian transmission mechanism believing that changes in the money stock operate only via investment and yet to believe that monetary factors dominate nominal income. This could occur in a situation of a high interest elasticity of investment. Conversely, one might believe that changes in the stock of money operate via the monetarist transmission mechanism affecting both consumption and investment and yet reject the quantity theory as an explanation of most observed changes in nominal income. This could occur where one views the total effect of changes in the money supply on consumption and investment as being small. So although the two monetarist propositions discussed so far are related, the structural parameters of the model used to analyse the economy and the specification of the model itself are crucial to the analysis of changes in nominal income.

This can be illustrated within the following model:

$$E = A + kY - ar. \qquad (1.2)$$

Aggregate real expenditure (E) is equal to an autonomous component (A), a component dependent on income (kY) and an interest sensitive component (ar). In equilibrium:

$$E = Y. \qquad (1.3)$$

In the money market the demand for real money balances M/P has a real income-dependent component (mY) and an interest-sensitive component (br), where r is the rate of interest.

$$\frac{M}{P} = mY - br. \qquad (1.4)$$

The supply of nominal money balances is assumed to be exogenously determined ($\bar{M}s$). In equilibrium:

$$\frac{M}{P} = \frac{\bar{M}s}{P}. \qquad (1.5)$$

Rearranging these relationships gives:

$$Y = \frac{1}{1 - \left(k - \frac{a}{b}m\right)} A + \frac{1}{m + \frac{b}{a}(1 - k)} \frac{\bar{M}s}{P}. \tag{1.6}$$

(See appendix 2 to this chapter for the derivation of equation 1.6.)

Within this framework traditional Keynesians would be characterised as low a and high b people. In the case where the ratio a/b is small, reference to equation 1.6 shows that the autonomous expenditure multiplier tends to $1/(1-k)$, while the money multiplier tends to zero. Disturbances from the real side of the economy would therefore be viewed by traditional Keynesians as dominating changes in nominal income.

On the other hand, monetarists would be characterised as high a and low b people. In the case where the ratio a/b is large reference again to equation 1.6 shows that the autonomous expenditure multiplier tends to zero while the money multiplier tends to $1/m$. Disturbances that are monetary in origin would therefore be viewed by monetarists as dominating changes in nominal income. (An alternative diagrammatic exposition using *IS* and *LM* curves is presented in appendix 3.)

1.4   The stability of the private sector

Another interrelated proposition that is part of the monetarist viewpoint is the contention that, if left to its own devices, the economy is inherently stable at a generally acceptable level of unemployment unless disturbed by erratic monetary growth. As examined in section 1.2.1, most (though not all) of the actually observed instability is attributed by monetarists to fluctuations in the money supply induced by the authorities. It is also held that the dynamic structure of the private sector is basically stable and that it absorbs shocks and transforms them into a stabilising motion.

In contrast to the monetarist viewpoint, Keynesian thought has rested on the assumption of an inherently unstable economy in which the authorities are supposed to be constantly active in offsetting swings in the level of economic activity. Traditional Keynesian analysis has regarded as the key to short-run economic movements a highly unstable marginal efficiency of investment schedule owing to shifts in business confidence, and a liquidity or money demand function that is highly elastic at low rates of interest and unstable at higher rates of interest. Modern Keynesians also contend that the economy is oscillatory and subject to fluctuations between long periods of unemployment and stagnation and periods of rapid expansion and inflation. The erratic shocks that cause these fluctuations are attributed primarily to changes in the marginal efficiency of investment, as the demand for money is treated by modern Keynesians as being fairly stable.

Monetarists and Keynesians differ not only on the major source of shocks affecting the economy but also on the length of time it takes to return to the neighbourhood of equilibrium once the economy has been subjected to a shock. Monetarists, because of their belief in a stable demand for money function, contend that, where the money supply is held on a stable growth path, real disturbances will be fairly rapidly absorbed and that output will revert back to its long-run growth path. They also believe that the business community's anticipations affecting their investment decisions are not subject to large swings independent of major policy changes pursued by the authorities. Modern Keynesians argue, however, that in the case of a disturbance the economy may take so long to return to the neighbourhood of equilibrium that this provides an additional rationale for short-run stabilisation actions with particular emphasis being given to the use of fiscal policy.

1.5 The irrelevance of allocative detail

The fourth basic analytical proposition of the monetarist viewpoint is the approximate separation of allocative (sectoral) and aggregative processes. Monetarists usually express little interest in allocative detail in explaining and predicting short-run changes in income. This view is related to the basic proposition embodied within the quantity theory and the monetarist version of the transmission mechanism. The belief that changes in the money stock are the predominant factor explaining changes in nominal income leads monetarists to concentrate on the behaviour of the market for real money balances. A sharp distinction is made between the general price level, which is affected by the quantity of money, and relative prices, which are affected by the particular market circumstances within the various sectors. It is asserted that substantial allocative detail yields only a marginal gain for predicting short-run changes in income as it is held that expenditures are determined mainly by an excess supply of or demand for real balances. This approximate separation of allocative and aggregative processes has helped to determine the monetarist preference for small-scale econometric models. This preference is further reinforced by the view that more weight should be attached to economic content and predictive power than to technical sophistication as such.

In contrast, Keynesians typically focus on what happens in particular sectors of the economy in trying to predict short-run changes in income. It is argued that expenditure motives in different sectors of the economy are crucial in analysing the aggregative performance of the economy. Importance is attached to the availability of credit and changing financial conditions (particularly various interest rates), as these are emphasised as influencing the volume of lending and borrowing and therefore expenditure. This interest in allocative detail has in turn helped to influence the research techniques employed by Keynesians. Large-scale econometric models have tended to be favoured as they provide detailed information on various sectors which they believe influence significantly the aggregative behaviour of the economy.

1.6 Concluding remarks

Having outlined the major theoretical propositions characterising the monetarist view, it should be apparent that they have strong implications for economic stabilisation policy. Before discussing monetarist policy prescriptions which are founded on empirical as well as theoretical bases in subsequent chapters, we will examine more fully the demand for money and the money supply process in chapters 2 and 3 respectively. A more detailed examination of the theoretical and empirical evidence on the demand for and supply of money is essential, owing to the importance attached to these relationships within monetarist analysis.

Appendix 1 : The Quantity Theory

$MV = PO$. If for example:

(1) M, the nominal money supply, = £60,000;

(2) V, the income velocity of money, = 5 (i.e., the number of times each pound on average circulates throughout the economy in exchange for newly produced real output);

(3) O, the real quantity of newly produced output, = 100,000 units;

(4) P, the average price of the newly produced real output, = £3.

Then $MV = PO$: £60,000 × 5 = £3 × 100,000.

Within this relationship velocity is equal to the inverse of the real quantity of money demanded per unit of output (k). This can be shown by either:

(a) the real quantity of money demanded is

$$\frac{Md}{P} = \frac{£60,000}{£3} = £20,000;$$

therefore with 100,000 units of output being produced the real quantity of money per unit of output produced equals $20,000/100,000 = 1/5$, $= k$. The inverse of $1/5$ i.e. $1/(1/5) = 5$, the income velocity of money; or,

(b) $MV = PO$; therefore $M = PO/V$. The demand for money Md is some fraction (k) of nominal income $Md = kPO$. In money market equilibrium $Md = M$; therefore $PO/V = kPO$. i.e. $V = 1/k$, remembering k is a fraction. Velocity is equal to the inverse of the real quantity of money demanded per unit of output.

Appendix 2: Algebraic Model

(1) $\qquad E = A + kY - ar.$ (1.2)

(2) In equilibrium, $E = Y$. (1.3)

(3) Therefore $Y = A + kY - ar.$

(4) $\qquad \dfrac{M}{P} = mY - br.$ (1.4)

(5) In equilibrium

$$\frac{M}{P} = \frac{\bar{M}s}{P}.$$ (1.5)

(6) Therefore
$$\frac{\bar{M}s}{P} = mY - br.$$

(7) $$br = mY - \frac{\bar{M}s}{P}.$$

(8) $$r = \left(mY - \frac{\bar{M}s}{P}\right)\frac{1}{b}.$$

(9) Substituting (8) into (3),
$$Y = A + kY - \frac{a}{b}\left(mY - \frac{\bar{M}s}{P}\right).$$

(10) Rearranging and multiplying out gives
$$Y - kY = A - \frac{a}{b}mY + \frac{a}{b}\frac{\bar{M}s}{P}.$$

(11) Rearranging and factorising gives
$$Y\left(1 - k + \frac{a}{b}m\right) = A + \frac{a}{b}\frac{\bar{M}s}{P}.$$

(12) Dividing through by

$$[1 - k + (a/b)m]$$

gives

$$Y = A\frac{1}{1 - k + (a/b)m} + \frac{a}{b}\frac{\bar{M}s}{P}\frac{1}{1 - k + (a/b)m}.$$

(13) Therefore
$$Y = A\frac{1}{1 - k + (a/b)m} + \frac{\bar{M}s}{P}\frac{1}{(b/a)(1 - k) + (b/a)(a/b)m}.$$

(14) Finally giving:
$$Y = A\frac{1}{1 - (k - (a/b)m)} + \frac{\bar{M}s}{P}\frac{1}{m + (b/a)(1 - k)}.$$
(equation (1.6) in the main text).

Appendix 3: Monetarists and Keynesians within The *IS – LM* Model

Within the *IS–LM* framework monetarists and Keynesians have tended to be distinguished by the relative slopes of the *IS* and *LM* curves. The *LM* curve will become steeper the more the demand for money is interest-inelastic, and flatter the more the demand for money is interest-elastic. The *IS* curve will become steeper the more investment and consumption are interest-inelastic, and flatter the more investment and consumption are interest-elastic.

Keynesians have been characterised as believing in a relatively flat *LM* curve and a relatively steep *IS* curve. This is illustrated in figures 1.1 and 1.2. Disturbances from the real side of the economy (shifts in the *IS* curve) are viewed by Keynesians as dominating changes in nominal income (figure 1.2).

On the other hand, monetarists have been characterised as believing in a relatively steep *LM* and a relatively flat *IS* curve. This is illustrated in figures 1.3 and 1.4. Disturbances that are monetary in origin (shifts in the *LM* curve) are viewed by monetarists as dominating changes in nominal income (figure 1.3).

It should be noted with regard to figures 1.1 and 1.3 that an expansionary monetary policy shifts the *LM* curve downwards to the right from LM_0 to LM_1, while in figures 1.2 and 1.4 an expansionary fiscal policy shifts the *IS* curve outwards to the right from IS_0 to IS_1. The extent to which the *LM* curve shifts will depend upon the interest elasticity of the demand for money and of course on the size of the monetary impulse. An increase in the supply of money will cause a small shift in the *LM* curve where the demand for money is relatively interest-elastic (figure 1.1), as equilibrium in the money market will be restored by a small fall in the rate of interest. In contrast, an identical increase in the money supply will cause a larger shift in the *LM* curve where the demand for money is relatively interest-inelastic (figure 1.3), as equilibrium in the money market will be restored only by a large fall in the rate of interest. Finally, it should be noted that in the case of a given expansionary fiscal impulse the *IS* curve shifts outwards to the right so that the horizontal distance is the same between the curves IS_0 and IS_1 in both figures 1.2 and 1.4.

Although certain aspects of monetarist views can be illustrated by using the *IS–LM* framework, it is inadequate as a framework for presenting monetarist views overall. For example, the slope properties of the curves do not contain all the relevant information for analysing the nature of the monetarist transmission mechanism (section 1.3.1),

Figure 1.1

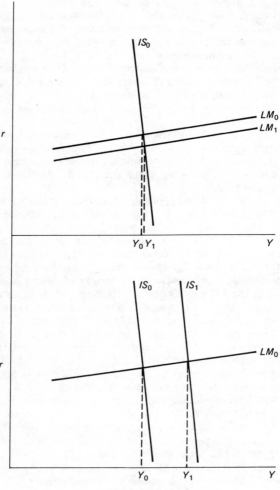

Figure 1.2

which suggests that money is a substitute over an array of financial and real assets and so any increase in the money supply would require not only an analysis of the slope properties of the curves but also an analysis of the simultaneous shifts of both curves (owing to substitution

Figure 1.3

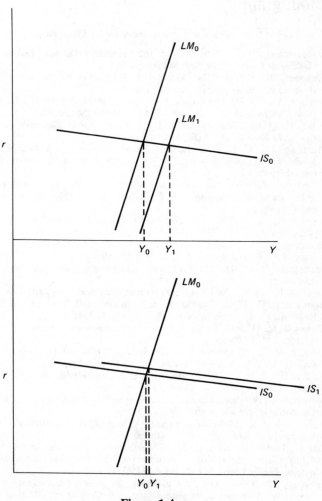

Figure 1.4

and wealth effects). The static *IS-LM* paradigm also suffers from a number of other inadequacies for presenting monetarist views overall with one of the weakest parts of the model being that it cannot accommodate simultaneous changes in prices and output and their interaction.

Bibliography

*Titles marked * are particularly recommended for student reading.*

*Andersen, L. (1973), 'The State of the Monetarist Debate'. *Federal Reserve Bank of St Louis Review*, vol. 56 (September).

*Brunner, K. (1970), 'The Monetarist Revolution in Monetary Theory'. *Weltwirtschaftliches Archiv*, vol. 105 (March).

Brunner, K. (1973), 'Commentary on the State of the Monetarist Debate'. *Federal Reserve Bank of St Louis Review*, vol. 56 (September).

Fand, D. (1970), 'Monetarism and Fiscalism'. *Banca Nazionale del Lavoro Quarterly Review*, no. 94 (September).

Friedman, M. (1956), 'The Quantity Theory of Money – A Restatement'. In *Studies in the Quantity Theory of Money*, edited by M. Friedman (Chicago: University Press).

*Friedman, M. (1968), 'Money: Quantity Theory'. In *International Encyclopedia of the Social Sciences*, edited by D. L. Sills, vol. 10 (New York: Macmillan and Free Press).

*Friedman, M. (1970), *The Counter-Revolution in Monetary Theory*. IEA Occasional Paper no. 33 (London: Institute of Economic Affairs).

Goodhart, C. A. E. and Crockett, A. D. (1970), 'The Importance of Money'. *Bank of England Quarterly Bulletin*, vol. 10 (June).

Harrington, R. (1971), 'The Monetarist Controversy'. *The Manchester School* (December).

Hicks, J. R. (1974), *The Crisis in Keynesian Economics*. (Oxford: Blackwell.)

*Johnson, H. G. (1971), 'The Keynesian Revolution and the Monetarist Counter-Revolution'. *American Economic Review*, vol. 61 (May).

Keynes, J. M. (1936), *The General Theory of Employment, Interest and Money*. (London: Macmillan.)

Klein, L. (1973), 'Commentary on the State of the Monetarist Debate'. *Federal Reserve Bank of St Louis Review*, vol. 56 (September).

*Laidler, D. E. W. (1971), 'Monetarism, Stabilisation Policy and the Exchange Rate'. *Banker's Magazine* (October).

Leijonhufvud, A. (1968), *On Keynesian Economics and the Economics of Keynes*. (London: Oxford University Press.)

*Leijonhufvud, A. (1969), *Keynes and the Classics*. IEA Occasional Paper no. 30 (London: Institute of Economic Affairs).

*Mayer, T. (1975), 'The Structure of Monetarism'. *Kredit und Kapital*, vol. 8.

Radcliffe Committee (1959), Committee on the Working of the Monetary System. *Report* Cmnd 827 (London: HMSO).

Samuelson, P. (1969), 'The Role of Money in National Economic Policy'. In *Controlling Monetary Aggregates*, Monetary Conference (Boston: Federal Reserve Bank of Boston).

Samuelson, P. (1971), 'Reflections on the Merits and Demerits of Monetarism'. In *Issues in Fiscal and Monetary Policy*, edited by J. Diamond (Chicago: De-Paul University).

Sayers, R. S. (1960), 'Monetary Thought and Monetary Policy in England'. *Economic Journal*, vol. 70 (December).

Schwartz, A. J. (1969), 'Why Money Matters'. *Lloyds Bank Review* (October).

Teigen, R. (1972), 'A Critical Look at Monetarist Economics'. *Federal Reserve Bank of St Louis Review*, vol. 54 (January).

2 The Demand for Money

In chapter 1 we discussed the importance of the stability of the velocity of circulation for the monetarist assertion that changes in the money supply are the main factor explaining changes in nominal income. The concept of velocity is closely linked to the demand for money function because, in equilibrium, where the demand for and supply of money are equal,

$$\frac{PO}{M} = V \tag{2.1}$$

(see appendix 1 to chapter 1). If the demand for money function is stable, then velocity would also be stable, changing in a predictable way if any of the arguments in the demand for money function should change.

Friedman (1956) has argued that the demand for money is highly stable in the sense that the quantity of money demanded can be predicted from a limited number of variables which appear in the demand for money function. This assertion is critical because, if the quantity of money demanded cannot be predicted accurately or if the number of variables appearing in the demand for money function is quite large, velocity would be unstable, and consequently it would be impossible to predict with any degree of accuracy the effect of an increase in the supply of money on the level of economic activity.

In this chapter then we shall examine in more detail the demand for money function, starting with a discussion of the traditional quantity theory of money and subsequently examining Keynesian liquidity preference theory together with post-Keynesian developments of this theory. Finally we shall look at the empirical evidence to see how far the monetarist assertion of a stable demand for money function can be substantiated. In all these discussions of the factors influencing the demand for money we shall examine only the influence of domestic variables. This is justified because, while noting that in theory the quantity of money demanded should depend on foreign variables such as the rate of interest in alternative financial centres, in practice economies are open mainly for current account transactions. There are many obstacles, both natural and man-made, to capital account transactions, and thus the influence of foreign variables on domestic money demand, while there, is likely to be attenuated.

2.1 The traditional quantity theory of money

In its traditional format, the quantity theory of money is a body of doctrine concerned with the relationship between the money supply and the general price level. Although the theory has taken a variety of forms, two formulations have had the most influence on modern thinking. They are the transactions version and the cash balance approach.

2.1.1 *The transactions version*

The transactions version is best analysed by first discussing the fundamental equation of exchange:

$$MV \equiv PT. \tag{2.2}$$

In this identity M, the quantity of money in circulation, times V, the transactions velocity of money, is by definition equal to P, the average price level of all transactions, times T, the number of transactions that take place. Therefore

$$V \equiv \frac{PT}{M} \tag{2.3}$$

so that the transactions velocity of money is equal to the average number of times money changes hands to finance all transactions (i.e. both final and intermediate).

Irving Fisher's transactions version of the quantity theory can be analysed by specifying the determinants of the variables within the identity (2.2). The nominal stock of money (M) was assumed to be exogenously determined by the monetary authorities (therefore independent of V, P and T) and at any point of time could be taken as given. The transactions velocity of money (V) was treated as being independent of M, P and T and was held to be determined by institutional arrangements (e.g. the length of the payments period). These institutional factors were thought to change only slowly over time, so that, for any short period of time, V could be treated as a constant. Turning to the right-hand side of the identity (2.2), T was also taken as given in the short run since the volume of transactions would be related in a fixed ratio to the level of output that classical economists held would always tend towards a position of full employment. With V and T taken as constant in the short run, the average price level of all transactions (P) would be determined solely by the quantity of money in circulation. Any increase in the money supply by the monetary authorities would then result in a proportionate rise in the general price level. This can be easily demonstrated by manipulating Fisher's formulation of the quantity theory:

$$MV = PT \qquad (2.4)$$

$$P = \frac{V}{T} M \qquad (2.5)$$

$$P = bM \qquad (2.6)$$

where b is a constant since V and T are assumed to be constant. Differentiating totally gives

$$dP = bdM \qquad (2.7)$$

Dividing both sides by $P \ (= b \ M)$:

$$\frac{dP}{P} = \frac{bdM}{bM} . \qquad (2.8)$$

Therefore the proportionate rate of change of prices exactly equals the proportionate rate of change of the money supply.

2.1.2   *The classical economic system*

The quantity theory outlined above was an essential ingredient of the working of the classical economic system. In the short run, with land, capital stock and the state of technology assumed to be constant, the level of output was held to be determined by the level of employment. Classical economists believed that, with flexible money wage rates and prices, full employment equilibrium (i.e. a situation where the quantity of labour demanded equals that supplied at the ruling real wage rate) would be achieved in the competitive labour market.

Say's Law, whereby supply creates its own demand, ruled out the possibility of a general insufficiency of demand, so that aggregate supply would equal aggregate demand. The law was believed to hold not only for a barter economy, but also for an exchange economy where money serves as a medium of exchange overcoming the inconvenience of barter. In an exchange economy the only reason for holding money would be to bridge the gap between the receipt of income and expenditure on goods and services. Any increase in income from the sale of goods or services would be matched by an equal increase in spending on goods and services. Savings would be deposited with financial institutions, where they could earn a rate of interest, and these savings would in turn be channelled into investment expenditure. Any imbalance between full employment savings and investment would therefore automatically be corrected by changes in the rate of interest. The full employment level of output would, as a result, be distributed between the production of consumption and capital goods.

In summary, the level of output was viewed as being determined by real factors (e.g. the demand for and supply of labour, the capital stock, etc.), and in consequence classical economists argued that money was neutral and that any change in the money supply would have no significant effect on such real variables as the real wage rate, the real rate of interest, investment, output and employment. The classical economists thereby dichotomised the pricing process by determining relative prices in the goods market and absolute prices in the money market. (For a more detailed examination of the classical model see any standard undergraduate macroeconomics textbook).

2.1.3 *The cash balance approach*

The second formulation of the quantity theory that has had a major influence on modern thinking is the Cambridge cash balance approach, attributed to Marshall and Pigou. This can be formulated in terms of the relationship:

$$MV = Py \qquad (2.9)$$

where P is the general price level appropriate to final output, as opposed to the general price level associated with all transactions analysed by Fisher; y is real income (final output); V is the income velocity of circulation of money, in contrast to Fisher's transactions velocity of money; and M is the quantity of money.

This formulation of the quantity theory was derived from an analysis of the demand for money at the microeconomic level and involved an examination of the factors that might be important in influencing an individual's demand for money. Within this approach what mattered was the real as opposed to the nominal quantity of money held. The demand for money was assumed, in consequence, to be proportional to the general price level, or equivalently as being a demand for real money balances. The determinants of the demand for real balances were viewed as being the volume of real transactions, or the level of real income or wealth. Owing to Pigou's use of the concept of resources, there is an ambiguity as to whether he was referring to transactions, income or wealth. However, the analysis was simplified by assuming that, for an individual and hence for the aggregate of individuals in an economy, the level of wealth, the level of income and the volume of transactions would bear a stable proportionate relationship to one another in the short run. The demand for nominal money balances was taken, *ceteris paribus*, to be proportional to the level of nominal income, so that:

$$Md = kPy. \qquad (2.10)$$

Therefore where equilibrium prevails in the money market and the demand for and supply of money are equal,

$$Md\,\frac{1}{k} = MV = Py \qquad (2.11)$$

giving the quantity theory formulation noted above in (2.10).

Pigou also viewed such factors as uncertainty about the future and some measure of the opportunity cost of holding money as influencing the demand for real balances (i.e. they would influence the size of k). Thus, by analysing the determinants of the amount of money a person desired to hold, the Cambridge approach permitted examination of variables that might affect the demand for money other than the institutional arrangements stressed by Fisher. However, like Fisher, Marshall and Pigou both analysed the relationship between the money supply and the general price level, as illustrated in figure 2.1.

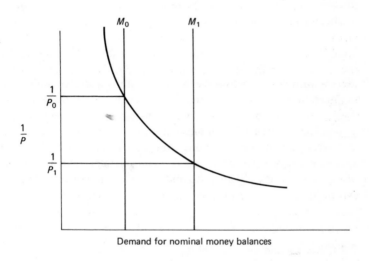

Demand for nominal money balances

Figure 2.1

In figure 2.1. the demand for nominal money balances is shown as a function of the inverse of the general price level. A curve of unit elasticity (rectangular hyperbola) will be traced out showing, *ceteris paribus*, the demand for nominal money as being proportional to the general price level. Equilibrium is achieved in the money market where the money supply, M_0 (exogenously determined by the authorities), is equal to the demand for money at a general price level of P_0. If the authorities increased the nominal money supply from M_0 to M_1, with the determinants of the demand for real balances (i.e. k and real income) held constant, the general price level would rise proportionately from P_0 to P_1, or in figure 2.1 the inverse of the general price level would fall from $1/P_0$ to $1/P_1$.

The position of the rectangular hyperbola would itself change if the variables affecting the demand for real balances changed. However, the value of such variables as the volume of real transactions, income, wealth and the rate of interest were still held to be determined by real as opposed to monetary factors. These variables were expected to change only slowly over time, so that in the short run the general price level would be determined by and proportional to the quantity of money. The Cambridge version of the quantity theory therefore preserved the neutrality of money, postulating a monetary theory of the general price level.

2.1.4   *Concluding remarks*

Before turning to discuss Keynesian liquidity preference theory, it is interesting to note that, in the two forms of the traditional quantity theory outlined above, money was generally seen as a substitute for goods and the transmission mechanism envisaged was therefore one of direct substitution of money for goods. However, within the quantity theory approach certain economists (in particular Thornton, Ricardo and Wicksell) analysed and discussed an indirect mechanism which linked money to prices via the rate of interest.

2.2   Keynes and the quantity theory

2.2.1   *Liquidity preference theory*

Keynes was concerned with the development of the Cambridge approach and subsequently analysed the motives that lead people to hold money. In the General Theory Keynes (1936) emphasised three main motives for holding money, namely the transactions, the precautionary and the speculative motives. The demand for money to carry out normal current transactions was subdivided between an income motive (for persons) and a business motive (for businesses). The demand for transactions balances was considered to be mainly dependent on and to be proportional to the level of income, and was derived from the function that money serves as a medium of exchange. The precautionary motive was to provide for unforeseen circumstances and also 'to hold an asset of which the value is fixed in terms of money to meet a subsequent liability fixed in terms of money' (Keynes, 1936). The demand for precautionary balances was also seen to be largely dependent upon the level of income. Lastly, the speculative motive was held to be due to uncertainty about the future level of the rate of interest (discussed more fully below). Keynes (1937) also postulated a finance motive which he held was related to expected/planned activity (spending). For example, money balances could be held by a firm wishing to finance a planned investment programme in the future. (Similar examples can be derived for households.) It should be noted that Keynesian analysis has tended to disregard this motive.

In his analysis Keynes focused attention on two alternative ways of holding financial assets: money whose value was fixed given the assumption of a stable price level, and long-term bonds, whose value would vary with changes in the rate of interest. In order to clarify this point, consider the example of a £1000 perpetual bond (i.e. one with no redemption date) issued with a fixed rate of interest of 5 per cent per annum. This would generate an income stream of £50 per annum. If, however, the rate of interest on new bonds is raised to 10 per cent, this would provide an income stream of £100 per annum for each £1000 bond. Clearly, the new bonds would be relatively more attractive and individuals would therefore try to sell the old bonds and invest the proceeds in new bonds. This would cause the market price of the old bonds to fall and equilibrium would be re-established when the price for old bonds was £500 (i.e. £50/£500× 100 = 10%). Conversely if the rate of interest on new bonds falls to 2½ per cent, then individuals would be willing to pay up to £2000 for bonds offering £50 per annum in perpetuity (i.e. £50/£2000 × 100 = 2½%). Hence it can be seen that the price of bonds varies inversely with the rate of interest.

In Keynes's analysis the demand for speculative balances depended upon the relationship between the current level of the rate of interest and the level of interest regarded as normal. A person's decision to allocate his wealth between either bonds or money would depend upon his expectations about the future rate of interest in relation to the level regarded as normal. Keynes postulated that different people would have different expectations about the future course of the rate of interest and he was able, in consequence, to postulate an aggregate speculative demand for money function which was a smooth and negative function of the current level of the rate of interest (figure 2.2).

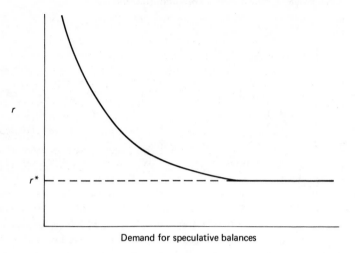

Demand for speculative balances

Figure 2.2

As rates of interest fall relative to the normal level, so more and more individuals would expect the rate of interest to rise. As we have shown, the price of bonds varies inversely with the rate of interest, so more individuals would have a preference for money as they would anticipate that the capital losses on their bond holdings would outweigh the small yield that could be earned on bonds. Conversely, as rates of interest rise relative to the normal level, more individuals would wish to hold bonds and there would be a small demand for speculative money balances. Not only could a high rate of interest be earned on bond holdings, but also individuals expecting the rate of interest to fall would anticipate a capital gain on their bond holdings. Following Friedman (1970), Keynes's liquidity preference function can be formalised as:

$$\frac{M^d}{P} = ky + f(r - r^e; r^e) \tag{2.12}$$

where M^d/P = real quantity of money demanded; ky = transactions and precautionary demand for money derived directly from the Cambridge cash balance approach; $f(\quad)$ = speculative demand; r = current market rate of interest; and r^e = expected or normal rate of interest.

2.2.2 *The Keynesian transmission mechanism*

Within this approach the equilibrium rate of interest is determined by equality between the quantity of money demanded and that supplied given the level of income. Thus the Keynesian demand for money function implies a transmission mechanism in which changes in the money supply lead to changes in the rate of interest, which in their turn alter the level of investment because the opportunity cost of funds necessary to finance investment has changed. Money in this transmission mechanism is seen purely as a substitute for financial assets, as compared with the direct substitution of money for goods generally envisaged by the traditional quantity theory approach.

2.2.3 *Two important theoretical possibilities*

Keynes's analysis implied two important theoretical possibilities. First, it implied that the relationship between the demand for money and the market rate of interest might be unstable over time. If, for example, individuals' views with regard to what constitutes a normal level of the rate of interest changed, so too would the real quantity of money demanded at any particular rate of interest. Second, at low rates of interest, which would be expected to prevail in conditions of underemployment equilibrium, the demand for money could become perfectly elastic with respect to the rate of interest as illustrated by the horizontal section of the liquidity preference schedule at r^* in figure 2.2. This has been termed the liquidity trap, as at r^* the rate of interest is so low that everyone expects it to rise so that they would be either unwilling to hold bonds (the expected capital loss outweighing interest received) or indifferent between money and bonds (the expected capital loss being matched by the interest received). With regard to the liquidity trap, it is interesting to note that, while Keynes himself put it forward only as a theoretical possibility and even said that he was not aware of it ever having been operative in practice, traditional Keynesian analysis has tended to associate an unstable demand for money function with the existence of the liquidity trap. Keynesians have argued that, in conditions of underemployment equilibrium, the demand for money would be unstable so that it would not be possible to predict accurately the quantity of money demanded from the arguments in the demand for money function (i.e. real income and the rate of interest).

2.2.4 *Offsetting movements in velocity*

Keynesians have traditionally belittled the role of monetary policy compared with that played by fiscal policy by specifying a relatively steep *IS* curve and a relatively flat *LM* curve (see appendix 3 to chapter 1). By analysing the two extreme cases of either a horizontal *LM* curve (where the demand for money becomes perfectly elastic with respect to the rate of interest) or a vertical *IS* curve (where consumption and investment are perfectly interest-inelastic), it can be shown that any change in the money supply would be exactly and completely offset by an opposite change in velocity so that monetary policy would be ineffective in influencing economic activity.

In the liquidity trap, illustrated in figure 2.3, any increase in the money supply would be absorbed entirely into idle/speculative balances. In such a situation an expansionary monetary policy would be incapable of reducing the rate of interest below r^*. At an unchanged level of income velocity would fall (i.e. the demand for money would be unstable).

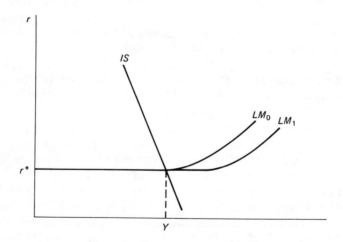

Figure 2.3

Alternatively, where consumption and investment are completely interest-inelastic, as illustrated in figure 2.4, again an increase in the money supply would have no effect on the level of real income. To maintain equilibrium in the money market, so that the increased supply of money is willingly held, the rate of interest would fall, and velocity would fall as the demand for money would rise relative to the unchanged level of income. In this case, even though the

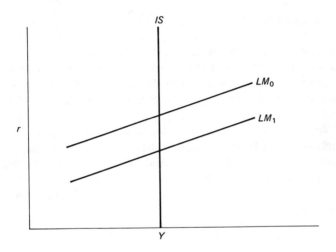

Figure 2.4

money demand function is stable, money is powerless to influence real variables because they are not sensitive to interest rate changes.

2.2.5 *Concluding remarks*

Keynesian liquidity preference theory, through its recognition of the fact that money is an asset that can be held as a store of value, has led quite naturally to an examination of how wealth is allocated among various assets (i.e. the development of portfolio theory). In this context, money is just one asset and excess money holdings will lead to the purchase of other assets, thus altering the relative prices of the various assets until such time as equilibrium is re-established. While this type of transmission mechanism is acceptable to both monetarists and non-monetarists alike, significant differences of opinion remain with regard to the range of assets that are considered to be substitutes for money. In section 2.3 we shall discuss the view advocated by the Yale School under the leadership of J. Tobin and in section 2.4 we consider Friedman's restatement of the quantity theory.

2.3   The demand for money: the New View

In the New View, the crucial difference is not between the banking sector and the rest of the economy but rather between the financial and the real sector (Tobin, 1969). It is impossible therefore to examine the demand for money in isolation from the rest of the financial sector. Money is not unique and there is a wide range of close substitutes for money such as deposits with non-bank financial intermediaries (NBFIs) and other short-term liquid assets (e.g. Treasury bills in the UK). The demand for money is influenced by the returns on all these other assets and is, therefore, not stable because of the large number of variables that appear in the demand for money function.

2.3.1   *Portfolio adjustment and the transmission mechanism*

Neo-Keynesian analysis has provided a generalised theory of portfolio selection by extending the portfolio choice from money and bonds to one involving more than these two assets. In the analysis money is seen as being only one of several forms in which wealth can be held. These alternatives include not only bonds (which bear a fixed interest but whose capital value varies inversely with the rate of interest) but also, for example, deposits with financial institutions (which bear an interest but whose capital value is fixed in nominal terms) and equities (which provide a variable return).

In contrast to traditional Keynesian analysis of the transmission mechanism, which has emphasised the bond yield in determining the cost of capital to firms, Tobin has emphasised the role played by the equity yield relative to the supply price of capital in influencing investment. Since within the New View money is a close substitute for financial assets, any increase in the money supply will cause individuals to dispose of their excess money holdings by purchasing these assets. This will tend to raise the price of financial assets including equities and, therefore, lower their yields. This rise in the price of equities will introduce a discrepancy between the market value of assets (as revealed by the equity price) and the cost of producing similar new assets, and this will increase the demand for capital equipment. For example, if an increase in the money supply raises the price of equities (i.e. reduces the yield on equities, called the return on capital) so that capital equipment that could be reproduced for £15,000 is valued at £20,000 in the equity market, then this gap would stimulate investment in new capital equipment. The stock market, therefore, provides a vital role in Tobin's analysis of the transmission mechanism. It is perhaps surprising though that an approach that lays such emphasis on modelling the entire financial sector should stress so strongly that particular channel of the transmission mechanism that occurs via changes in the market price of equities (i.e. the return on capital).

However, a further channel for the transmission mechanism is quite compatible with either Keynesian or neo-Keynesian analysis. If, as is likely, the financial markets are not perfectly competitive, then monetary changes may cause credit rationing, which in turn will influence aggregate demand and, therefore, output and employment. This arises because rates of interest are not freely determined by demand and supply but rather by the financial institutions operating in the markets, so that the rates will be slow to respond to changes in the underlying market conditions. The financial institutions will, therefore, be forced to ration credit, or conversely to relax the stringency of credit rationing if the market change is expansionary. In this case the quantity of credit available is not limited by the amount borrowers would wish to obtain at the ruling rates of interest but rather by the amount made available to them by the financial institutions.

2.4 Friedman's restatement of the quantity theory

2.4.1 *A theory of the demand for money*

Friedman (1956) presented his restatement of the quantity theory of money as, in the first instance, a theory of the demand for money, rather than a theory of output, or of nominal income or of the price level. Within the modern quantity theory the demand for money is treated like the demand for a durable good. Durable goods provide a flow of services from which ultimate wealth-holders derive utility. It is asserted that money also yields a flow of services (hence utility) to the holder and consequently money is treated as an asset, with the demand for money analysed as a demand for a stock. There are a variety of services that an individual may receive from holding money and these include: convenience, consumption services (as money is a readily available source of purchasing power), services from its market value being generally highly predictable, pride of possession, a reserve for the future and services by providing a feeling of security to the holder of money.

The demand for money (like the demand for any asset) will depend upon three major factors: (1) the wealth constraint, which will determine the maximum amount of money that can be held; (2) the yield on money in relation to the yield on other assets in which wealth can be held; and (3) the asset-holder's tastes and preferences.

Although wealth (W) is considered the appropriate constraint on money-holding, Friedman broadened the concept to include human wealth. Non-human wealth consists of a stock of assets (e.g. bonds and durable goods) which can be sold and the proceeds devoted to holding wealth entirely in the form of money. An individual could also theoretically sell a claim to his future income stream from work and likewise devote the proceeds to holding money (human wealth being the capital value of this stream). However, although it is possible to buy and sell non-human wealth, in the absence of slavery there is no market for human capital. As a result, in specifying the demand for money function Friedman included the ratio of human to non-human wealth (w) as a subsidiary variable, anticipating that, *ceteris paribus*, the higher the human component for a given stock of wealth, the larger the demand for money to compensate for the lack of marketability of human wealth.

Friedman distinguished five forms in which wealth could be held: in money, bonds, equities, physical goods and human capital. The way total wealth is allocated between the various forms will depend upon the relative rates of return on the various assets. Money yields a return in kind owing to the services that are derived from holding it. However, there is also a real yield on money holdings which will depend upon movements in the price level (P). If the price level rises, the real value of nominal balances falls so that holders of money would experience a capital loss in real terms and vice versa. The demand for nominal balances, therefore, becomes a function of the price level (P).

The return on bonds takes the form of an interest income received by the bond-holder (r_b) and also any change in the price of the bond over time ($(1/r_b)(dr_b/dt)$). As the price of income-earning assets, like bonds, varies inversely with the rate of interest, the expected percentage rate of change of the rate of interest is subtracted from the rate of interest return on bonds, as it is opposite in sign to the expected percentage rate of capital gain and loss. The rate of return on equities can take three forms: a nominal amount per year (r_e), an addition or subtraction to the nominal amount to adjust for changes in prices ($(1/P)(dP/dt)$), and any change in the nominal price of the equity over time ($(1/r_e)(dr_e/dt)$). Physical goods yield not only a return, or income in kind, by providing a flow of services to their owners, but also a nominal return in the form of any appreciation or depreciation in their money value ($(1/P)(dP/dt)$).

The final form in which, according to Friedman, wealth could be held is in human capital. However, owing to the difficulty of measuring the rate of return on such investment, the ratio of human to non-human wealth (w) is included in the demand for money function. Finally in the function, u, stands for any variables that can be expected to affect tastes and preferences. In wartime, for example, uncertainty may cause individuals to want to hold a larger fraction of their wealth in the form of money. However, tastes and preferences are generally taken for granted and assumed constant both over time and space. This gives then a demand for money function of the following form:

$$Md = f\left(P, r_b - \frac{1}{r_b}\frac{dr_b}{dt}, r_e + \frac{1}{P}\frac{dP}{dt} - \frac{1}{r_e}\frac{dr_e}{dt}, \frac{1}{P}\frac{dP}{dt}; w; W; u\right) \qquad (2.13)$$

where (1) P, represents the price level;

    (2) $\left.\begin{array}{c} r_b \\ r_e \end{array}\right\}$ represent the rate of return on bonds and equities;

    (3) $(1/P)(dP/dt)$, represents the expected rate of inflation;

    (4) w represents the ratio of human to non-human wealth;

    (5) W represents total wealth;

    (6) u represents tastes; and

    (7) derivatives denote expected rates of change.

The form of the function outlined above is often simplified in the following manner. First of all, the function is assumed to be homogeneous of degree one in prices so that the demand for money becomes a demand for real balances (M/P). Second, by abstracting from capital gains and losses, the returns on bonds and equities can be represented by r_b and r_e respectively. Third, the return on money can be incorporated into the analysis by introducing r_m into the function. Finally, because of the difficulties of measurement, Friedman's more inclusive wealth concept (incorporating human wealth) has been proxied by a measure of permanent income (y^p), using an exponentially weighted average of current and past levels of income, with w in the function representing the fraction of wealth in non-human form. Thus the function can be written (Friedman, 1970):

$$\frac{M^d}{P} = f(\underbrace{y^P, w}_{a}; \underbrace{r_m, r_b, r_e, \frac{1}{P}\frac{dP}{dt}}_{b}; \underbrace{u}_{c}) \tag{2.14}$$

where (1) a represents the budget constraint;
      (2) b represents the return on money and competing assets; and
      (3) c represents individual preferences.

It should be noted that money will also be demanded by business enterprises, but Friedman suggests that recognition of this fact will not alter the above demand for money function to any great extent.

Patinkin (1969) has argued that Friedman's restatement is merely an elegant exposition of the modern Keynesian portfolio approach to the demand for money; but, while Friedman has admitted that Keynesian liquidity preference analysis has much influenced his work, one important difference exists between the two approaches. In the restatement Friedman (2.13) introduced the expected rate of inflation as a potentially important variable into the demand for money function, whereas in contrast Keynesian portfolio balance theory invariably assumes either a stable actual or expected price level. However, the faster prices rise, the more rapidly the real value of money falls, so that a positive rate of inflation generates a negative yield on money balances. Friedman thus predicted an inverse relationship between the demand for real balances and the expected rate of inflation.

2.4.2 *Portfolio adjustment and the transmission mechanism*

The variables specified in the demand for money function indicate the rate of return that can be earned by holding assets other than money. Consequently the variables measure the opportunity cost of holding money, that is the return that is forgone if money rather than other assets is held. Within this analysis holders of money will adjust their holdings of money balances if the rate of return on other forms in which wealth can be held should change. The analysis, therefore, predicts that the demand for money will fall, *ceteris paribus*, if the yield on other assets rise, and vice versa. Individuals will allocate wealth between the different assets to equalise marginal rates of return, thereby maximising their utility. If marginal rates of return are not equal, a reallocation of wealth between assets would take place.

This portfolio adjustment process is central to the monetarist specification of the transmission mechanism. This can be illustrated by examining the effects of an increase in the money supply arising from an open market purchase of government securities by the authorities. The initial situation is assumed to be an equilibrium position where wealth is allocated between assets such that the marginal rates of return are equal. In order to persuade wealth-holders to exchange government securities for money balances, the price of these securities would have to rise and the yield, therefore, fall. Owing to the open market operations the public's money holdings will rise relative to its holdings of financial and real assets. As the marginal return on any asset diminishes as holdings of it increase, the marginal rate of return on money holdings, relative to other assets, will fall. Consequently, the public's holdings of money balances will be greater than their desired level. In order to bring marginal rates of return back into equilibrium, a reallocation of wealth will take place between assets, which will involve alterations of stocks of both financial and non-financial assets. As excess money balances are exchanged for financial and real assets, their relative prices will be changed. The price of real assets will tend to rise and interest rates on financial assets will tend to fall.

The role of relative prices in the transmission mechanism has been stressed in particular by Brunner and Meltzer, who divide output into four categories: consumption goods, and type I, II and III capital goods. Type I capital goods are those that have separate market prices for existing stock (through equity prices) and new stock, and the transmission mechanism here is identical to that discussed in section 2.3.1 above. In contrast, type II capital goods have a single price for new output and existing stock of comparable quality (e.g. housing), and the rise in the price of existing assets consequent upon the monetary expansion would lead, *ceteris paribus*, to increases in the production of these assets. Finally, type III assets are those for which there is virtually no market for existing assets or claims to them (e.g. certain consumer durables such as washing machines). The private sector's expenditure both on this type of asset and also on consumer goods will increase in response to the rise in the market value of aggregate wealth following the rise in the price of capital goods and also financial securities (owing to the fall in interest rates). This portfolio adjustment process will then impinge upon a wide array of assets and as a result, either directly or indirectly, spending will increase on a wide range of goods and services. While both monetarists and neo-Keynesians argue that monetary impulses are transmitted to the real economy through a portfolio adjustment process, they disagree on the range of assets and associated expenditures considered. Monetarists stress a much broader range of assets (financial and real) and associated expenditures than do neo-Keynesians, and in consequence attribute a much stronger effect on aggregate spending to monetary impulses.

2.5   The modern quantity theory: predictions concerning nominal income

Although the modern quantity theory may be in the first instance a theory of the demand for money, the additional assumptions necessary to make predictions about nominal income and the price level are invariably made. At the heart of the theory is the assertion that there exists a stable functional relationship between the demand for real balances and a limited number of variables. It is the functional relationship (i.e. behaviour), between the quantity of money demanded and the variables that determine it, that is held to be stable, so that changes in the demand for money would occur if any of the variables in the demand for money function should change. Velocity is not regarded as being a numerical constant over time. Therefore in order to turn the restated quantity theory into a model of income determination, it is necessary to make one of either of two assumptions. First, that the demand for money is inelastic with respect to the variables that determine it. In such circumstances the percentage change in the amount of money demanded to given percentage changes in the variables determining it would be small so that movements in velocity would also be small. However, if the variables influencing the demand for money are themselves subject to large variations, large changes in the demand for money and velocity could also occur, and this could invalidate accurate predictions of the effect of changes in the money supply on nominal income. Second, that the variables affecting the demand for money are taken as fixed or determined elsewhere aside from monetary forces. Monetarists express the view, as evidenced by Friedman (1968), that both the real rate of interest and real income are determined by real and not by monetary forces. In chapter 4 we shall discuss this assertion and also the way in which changes in nominal income are divided between changes in output and the price level following a change in the money supply. This will involve a discussion of the importance of price expectations and the distinction between short- and long-run effects. In terms of the quantity theory relationship, monetarists argue that empirical evidence has shown that changes in velocity are relatively minor compared with changes in the money supply and that, rather than offsetting movements in the money supply, changes in velocity in point of fact reinforce them. It is to the empirical evidence on the demand for money that we now turn.

2.6 Empirical evidence

Empirical studies on the demand for money have been able to throw light on the question of which variables influence the demand for money and also whether the relationship between the demand for money and these variables are stable over time. In this section we shall only briefly summarise the main findings from the empirical studies on the demand for money. A fuller discussion of both the theories and empirical evidence on the demand for money can be found in Laidler (1977).

2.6.1   *Summary of main empirical findings*

In the large number of studies that have now been carried out most researchers have employed a demand for money function of the following form:

$$\frac{Md}{P} = aX^{\beta_1} r^{\beta_2} \tag{2.15}$$

where X refers to the constraint on holding money and r to the rate of interest. In most of the studies the money supply has been defined either as currency plus demand deposits at commercial banks (narrow definition) or as currency plus demand and time deposits at commercial banks (broad definition); X has been defined as either the level of wealth, the level of income or the level of permanent income; and r as short- or long-term interest rates. The elasticity with respect to $X(\beta_1)$ and $r(\beta_2)$ has then been estimated via regressions of different definitions of money on various definitions and combinations of X and r. The main findings from the empirical studies can be briefly summarised as follows.

(1) On the question of the most appropriate constraint on holding money, wealth rather than current income appears to be the appropriate constraint as it has been found to explain more of the variation in the demand for money than has current income. This particular finding is invariant as to how money, wealth or the rate of interest have been defined. Friedman's more inclusive wealth concept (incorporating human wealth) has been proxied in a number of studies by a measure of permanent income using an exponentially weighted average of current and past levels of income. However, although the evidence indicates that wealth is the appropriate constraint on money holdings, it is inconclusive as to whether it should include or exclude human wealth.

(2) On the question of the stability of the demand for money with respect to the rate of interest, the evidence points strongly to the demand for money being stably and negatively related to the rate of interest, with little evidence supporting the existence of the

liquidity trap. The numerical value for the interest elasticity of the demand for money has varied depending upon both the choice of the definition of the rate of interest and that of the money supply employed in the studies. For American studies on annual data the general pattern has been:

(a) $M_1 + r_L$ −0.7 to −1.10

(b) $M_2 + r_L$ −0.45 to −0.75

(c) $M_1 + r_S$ −0.20 to −0.45

(d) $M_2 + r_S$ −0.00 to −0.20

where M_1 and M_2 refer to narrow and broad definitions of money respectively and r_s and r_L to short- and long-term representative rates of interest.

(3) The expected rate of inflation has generally been found to be an important variable in times of hyperinflation but not in times of mild inflation. However the rate of interest used in the regressions has normally been the nominal rate which itself may be expected to vary directly with the expected rate of inflation (see chapter 4). Thus, in the estimation of the money demand function, the coefficient for the normal rate of interest may be picking up the effects on the demand for money of both interest rates and the expected rate of inflation.

(4) Finally, empirical evidence has supported the specification of the demand for money in real terms, thereby confirming the hypothesis that, *ceteris paribus*, the demand for money is proportional to the price level.

Monetarists argue that the results from empirical studies, summarised above, indicate that there exists a stable relationship between the demand for real money balances and a few variables, particularly the rate of interest and wealth. Stable demand for money functions have been found using both narrow and broad definitions of money.

However, empirical evidence on the stability of the demand for money is neither as clear-cut nor as uncontroversial as is often suggested. In the United Kingdom, a number of recent studies (e.g. Hacche, 1974; Artis and Lewis, 1974, 1976) have found evidence of apparent instability of the demand for money function since the introduction of Competition and Credit Control in September 1971. It should be noted that evidence of instability (or for that matter of stability) could also arise from a mis-specification of the demand for money function. Consequently, it would be incorrect to conclude automatically that the inability to identify a stable relationship, using traditional specifications, precludes the possible existence of a stable demand for money function. Artis and Lewis (1976), for example, have shown that it is possible to identify a relatively stable demand function for the UK when the function is reformulated to make the money supply exogenous. A stable demand for money function, with a narrow definition of money employed, has also been identified for the UK by Coghlan (1978). In contrast to the approach adopted in many previous studies, Coghlan allowed for a different time lag in the adjustment of money balances to changes in the various explanatory variables. For the United States, Hamburger (1977) has suggested that the instability identified by some demand for money functions since 1974 may well be the result of the restrictive specifications of the functions employed in which the opportunity cost variables have been inappropriately chosen.

In conclusion, it would appear that a general consensus of opinion regarding the stability of the demand for money function is not as yet possible. Monetarists argue that the overwhelming body of empirical evidence indicates that the demand for money is a stable function of a limited number of variables and that evidence of apparent instability can be readily explained. Other economists still question whether the demand for money is stable enough to permit great reliance on monetary policy. Before examining the evidence on movements in velocity, a final point worth noting is that the attention given to monetary aggregates by monetarists also depends on the belief that the demand for money function is less unstable than the expenditure function (this aspect is discussed in chapter 5).

2.6.2 *Movements in velocity*

Given the monetarist belief that the demand for money is a stable function of a few variables, the question remains as to whether velocity changes in an offsetting and opposite direction to changes in the supply of money. Friedman and Schwartz (1963), in their study of the monetary history of the United States, found that the demand for real balances relative to real income had risen over time as income had risen whereas velocity had fallen secularly. In the period studied, 1869–1960, they found that the secular fall in velocity had occurred steadily, with the only major exceptions occurring during and after the contraction of the 1930s and the Second World War. During the nine decades covered between 1869 and 1960 velocity fell by an average of just over 1 per cent a year (trend). However in its cyclical pattern velocity was found either to rise or to decline at less than this rate during business expansions when real income was rising, and to decline at more than the average of 1 per cent a year during business contractions when real income was falling. Velocity was therefore found then to have a consistent cyclical pattern about its secular trend for the period studied.

2.6.3   Concluding remarks

Monetarists argue that short-run variations in velocity are relatively small compared with changes in the money supply and that such variations that take place reinforce, rather than offset, movements in the money supply. In such circumstances, it is argued that the authorities are in a strong position to influence the level of economic activity if they choose to control the money supply. In chapter 3 we shall then examine the money supply and the contention that the authorities can control the money supply if they choose to do so.

Bibliography

Titles marked * are particularly recommended for student reading.

Artis, M. J. and Lewis, M. K. (1974), 'The Demand for Money: Stable or Unstable?' *The Banker*, vol. 124 (March).
Artis, M. J. and Lewis, M. K. (1976), 'The Demand for Money in the United Kingdom: 1963–1973'. *The Manchester School*, vol. 44.
Brunner, K. (1971), 'A Survey of Selected Issues in Monetary Theory'. *Revue Suisse d'Economie Politique et de Statistique*, vol. 107.
Coghlan, R. T. (1978), 'A Transactions Demand for Money'. *Bank of England Quarterly Bulletin*, vol. 18 (March).
Friedman, M. (1956), 'The Quantity Theory of Money – A Restatement'. In *Studies in the Quantity Theory of Money*, edited by M. Friedman (Chicago: University Press).
Friedman, M. (1968), 'The Role of Monetary Policy'. *American Economic Review*, vol. 58 (March).
*Friedman, M. (1970), 'A Theoretical Framework for Monetary Analysis'. *Journal of Political Economy*, vol. 78, (March/April).

Friedman, M. (1972), 'Comments on the Critics'. *Journal of Political Economy*, vol. 80 (September/October).

Friedman, M. and Meiselman, D. (1963), 'The Relative Stability of Monetary Velocity and the Investment Multiplier in the United States, 1898–1958'. In *Commission on Money and Credit: Stabilization Policies* (Englewood Cliffs, NJ: Prentice/Hall).

Friedman, M. and Schwartz, A. J. (1963), *A Monetary History of the United States, 1867–1960* (Princeton: University Press).

Hacche, G. (1974), 'The Demand for Money in the United Kingdom: Experience Since 1971'. *Bank of England Quarterly Bulletin*, vol. 14 (September).

Hamburger, M. J. (1977), 'Behaviour of the Money Stock, Is There a Puzzle?' *Journal of Monetary Economics*, vol. 3 (July).

*Johnson, H. G. (1967), 'Recent Developments in Monetary Theory'. In *Essays in Monetary Economics*, edited by H. G. Johnson (London: George Allen & Unwin).

*Johnson, H. G. (1971), 'Recent Developments in Monetary Theory: A Commentary'. In *Money in Britain 1959–1969*, edited by D. R. Croome and H. G. Johnson (Oxford: University Press).

Keynes, J. M. (1936), *The General Theory of Employment, Interest and Money* (London: MacMillan).

Keynes, J. M. (1937), 'The Ex-Ante Theory of the Rate of Interest'. *Economic Journal*, vol. 47 (June).

Laidler, D. E. W. (1971), 'The Influence of Money on Economic Activity: A Survey of Some Current Problems'. In *Monetary Theory and Policy in the 1970s*, edited by C. Clayton, J. C. Gilbert and R. Sedgwick (London: Oxford University Press).

*Laidler, D. E. W. (1977), *The Demand for Money: Theories and Evidence*, 2nd ed. (New York: Dun-Donnelley Publishing Corp).

*Park, Y. C. (1972), 'Some Current Issues on the Transmission Process of Monetary Policy'. *International Monetary Fund, Staff Papers* (March).

Patinkin, D. (1969), 'The Chicago Tradition, the Quantity Theory and Friedman'. *Journal of Money, Credit and Banking*, vol. 1 (February).

Pigou, A. C. (1917), 'The Value of Money', *Quarterly Journal of Economics*, vol. 32 (November).

Tobin, J. (1969), 'A General Equilibrium Approach to Monetary Theory'. *Journal of Money, Credit and Banking*, vol. 1 (February).

3 The Supply of Money

In this chapter we will examine the theoretical analysis and empirical evidence on the supply of money, but first we shall start with a brief discussion of the problem of specifying the choice of assets to be included in the definition of money.

3.1 The definition of money

There is no generally accepted definition, among economists, as to what constitutes money. The controversy has largely been centred on whether to define the money supply as (1) currency in the hands of the public plus demand deposits at commercial banks; or (2) currency plus demand and time deposits (i.e. those for which notice of withdrawal must be given) at commercial banks; or (3) currency plus demand and time deposits plus the liabilities of non-bank financial intermediaries. Economists have been unable to produce a generally acceptable definition of money based on theoretical grounds.

Monetarists argue that the solution to the problem of the appropriate definition of money is an empirical matter. In their view the first and foremost consideration should be the use that can be made of such a definition in explaining and predicting the consequences of changes in the supply of and demand for money on important economic variables, such as real income, prices and interest rates. In chapter 2 it was noted that stable demand for money functions have been found for both narrow (currency plus demand deposits) and broad definitions of money (currency plus demand and time deposits). Monetarists argue that there is no need to include the liabilities of non-bank financial intermediaries in defining money since stable demand for money functions have been found without the inclusion of these liabilities. They also tend to be indifferent

between a narrow and a broad definition of money as they believe
that the authorities can control both the volume of currency and
the liabilities of the commercial banks. We will now turn to a discussion of the determination of the money supply.

3.2   The monetary base approach

Banks can increase the level of their deposits (and therefore the
money supply) by: (1) buying financial securities and/or (2) increasing their loans. Both of these methods increase their assets and
liabilities by equal amounts. The essence of the monetary base
approach is that there is a stable relationship between the quantity
of reserve assets available to the banks and the level of their deposits.
The authorities are assumed to determine the quantity of reserve
assets and the banks, as profit-maximisers, will ensure that the
volume of their deposits is equal to the so-called bank multiplier
times the volume of reserve assets. If additional reserve assets
become available, then the banks will seize the opportunity to
increase their profits by increasing deposits through buying financial
securities or increasing their loans until such time as the ratio
between deposits and reserve assets is restored to the specified level.
Monetarists assert that there is, therefore, a stable behavioural
relationship between the money supply and the stock of reserve
assets.

This analysis will now be presented in more detail within the
confines of a simple banking system. In this system the money supply
is defined as notes and coins (currency) held by the public outside
the banking system (C_p) and all deposits (D) of the private sector
with the banks (i.e. both demand and time deposits). Thus the
money supply:

$$M = C_p + D. \tag{3.1}$$

3.2.1   *The proximate determinants of the money supply*

In analysing the determination of the money supply the behaviour
of three sets of agents needs to be taken into account: that of the
monetary authorities, the banks and the public. The quantity of

notes and coins (referred to henceforth as high-powered money, H) is determined by the behaviour of the monetary authorities. Within the monetary base approach it is assumed that the authorities control the amount of high-powered money so that the stock of high-powered money is taken as given. This given quantity of high-powered money can be held by the banks (C_b) and by the public (C_p), so that

$$H = C_b + C_p. \tag{3.2}$$

The banks hold a fraction of deposits in the form of high-powered money (ρ, the reserve ratio) so that

$$C_b = \rho D. \tag{3.3}$$

The public also hold a fraction of their deposits in the form of high-powered money (λ, the currency ratio) so that

$$C_p = \lambda D. \tag{3.4}$$

Using the above equations we may set out the determination of the money supply more formally:

$$M = C_p + D \tag{3.1}$$

$$H = C_b + C_p \tag{3.2}$$

$$C_b = \rho D \tag{3.3}$$

$$C_p = \lambda D. \tag{3.4}$$

Dividing relationship (3.1) by (3.2) gives

$$\frac{M}{H} = \frac{C_p + D}{C_b + C_p}. \tag{3.5}$$

Substituting relationships (3.3) and (3.4) into (3.5) we obtain

$$\frac{M}{H} = \frac{\lambda D + D}{\rho D + \lambda D}. \tag{3.6}$$

Factorising gives

$$\frac{M}{H} = \frac{(1 + \lambda)D}{(\rho + \lambda)D}. \tag{3.7}$$

Finally cancelling out:

$$M = \frac{1 + \lambda}{\rho + \lambda} H. \tag{3.8}$$

The proximate determinants of the money supply are, therefore, the volume of high-powered money (H), the reserve ratio (ρ), and the currency ratio (λ). A rise in the volume of high-powered money, or a fall in either the reserve ratio or the currency ratio, will lead, *ceteris paribus*, to an increase in the money supply. Conversely, a fall in the volume of high-powered money, or a rise in either the reserve ratio or the currency ratio, will lead, *ceteris paribus*, to a decrease in the money supply.

3.2.2   *A diagrammatic presentation*

These results can be shown in the following diagrammatic presentation of the monetary base approach. In figure 3.1 the amount of high-powered money and its division between the total currency holdings of the banks and the public is shown on the vertical axis. The banks' share is measured downwards from A and the public's share upwards from O. The amount of deposits created by the banks is shown along the horizontal axis (OD) and this will depend on the reserve ratio and the banks' holding of high-powered money. The line AB therefore shows the relationship between the banks' holdings of reserve assets and the maximum quantity of deposits that can be created, with the absolute value of the slope being equal to the reserve–asset ratio (ρ). Finally, the line OC shows the public's demand for currency which increases as the level of deposits increases, the slope of OC being equal to the currency ratio (λ).

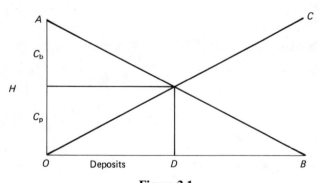

Figure 3.1

In the simple multiple-deposit-creation case, where the given quantity of high-powered money is held entirely by the banking system, so that the currency ratio is zero, the maximum amount of deposits that can be created is

$$D = \frac{1}{\rho} H. \qquad (3.9)$$

For example, in the case where the volume of high-powered money is £100 and this is held entirely by the banks (OA in figure 3.1) and the reserve ratio is 0.5, the maximum amount of deposits that can be created is equal to £200 (OB in figure 3.1). The multiple creation of deposits will be modified owing to the drain of cash out of the banks by the public as deposits increase. Where both the reserve and currency ratios are equal to 0.5 and the given quantity of high-powered money (£100) is divided equally between the public and the banks (i.e. £50 each), the maximum amount of deposits that can be created is equal to £100 (OD in figure 3.1). In such a situation equilibrium prevails as the plans of all economic agents are consistent with each other.

3.2.3   *Changes in the volume of high-powered money*

If the authorities increased the volume of high-powered money, then *ceteris paribus*, the money supply would increase. This result is illustrated in figure 3.2. The increase in the volume of high-

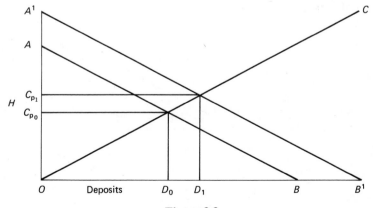

Figure 3.2

powered money is shown by a parallel shift outwards of the diagonal line AB to $A^1 B^1$. As a result the money supply increases as both of its component parts increase. The currency holdings of the public increase from OC_{p_0} to OC_{p_1}, and the deposits created by the banks increase from OD_0 to OD_1.

It should be noted that in figure 3.2 the ratio $(B\ B^1)/(A\ A^1)$ measures the simple bank multiplier on the assumption that the public's demand for cash remains constant; however, after allowing for the increased holdings of cash by the public, the multiplier is

$$\frac{C_{p_1} - C_{p_0} + D_1 - D_0}{AA^1}.$$

3.2.4 *Changes in the currency ratio*

A fall in the currency ratio will lead, *ceteris paribus*, to an increase in the money supply. This result is illustrated in figure 3.3. A fall in the currency ratio is shown diagrammatically by a reduction in the slope of the line OC, so that OC rotates to OC^1. This will reduce the public's share of the given total of high-powered money from OC_{p_0} to OC_{p_1}, thus increasing the banks' share to AC_{p_1}, permitting an expansion of their deposits from OD_0 to OD_1. Hence although one component (C_p) of the money supply decreases and the other increases (D), the overall effect will be an increase in the money supply because the rise in deposits will be greater than the fall in the public's currency holdings.

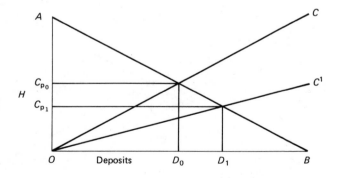

Figure 3.3

3.2.5 *Changes in the reserve ratio*

A fall in the reserve ratio will lead, *ceteris paribus*, to an increase in the money supply. This result is illustrated in figure 3.4. A fall in the reserve ratio is shown by a change in the position of line AB along the horizontal axis as a fall will allow a larger multiple creation of deposits. The line will pivot from AB to AB^1. As both the currency holdings of the public increase from OC_{p_0} to OC_{p_1} and deposits increase from OD_0 to OD_1, the total money supply will increase.

3.2.6 *Empirical evidence*

Using the monetary base approach, the contribution of these proximate determinants to changes in the money supply has been examined in a number of studies, notably by Sheppard (1971) for the UK, Friedman and Schwartz (1963b) and Cagan (1965) for the United States. The approach followed in these studies was to estimate the hypothetical changes in the money supply 'that would have occurred if each of the determinants in turn changed as it did while the others had remained at their initial level' (Friedman and Schwartz, 1963b).

Sheppard has estimated that the whole period, 1881–1962, the change in high-powered money (defined as currency outstanding plus bankers' and private deposits at the Bank of England) contributed 92 per cent of the change in the money supply in the UK, whereas changes in the currency and reserve ratios accounted for

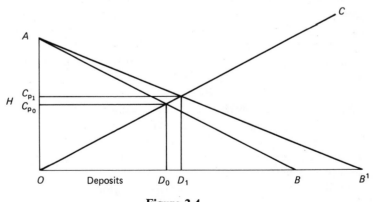

Figure 3.4

+10 per cent and —1 per cent respectively (the difference, i.e. —1 per cent, being due to the interaction of these factors; for a description of the methodology see Friedman and Schwartz, 1963b). In their study of the monetary history of the United States between 1867 and 1960, Friedman and Schwartz also found that changes in high-powered money were the major factor accounting for changes in the money supply over the whole period. They estimated that the change in high-powered money contributed 86 per cent of the change in the money supply in the United States between 1881–1960, while changes in the currency and reserve ratios contributed +3 and +9 per cent respectively. With regard to the movements of the currency and reserve ratios there are some similarities between the UK and US experience. In the pre-1914 period the currency ratio fell steadily in both countries, while both ratios moved in the same general direction in the 1920s and 1950s. Apart from these periods there are no other similarities. In the post-1920 period movements in the US ratios have been substantially larger and their trends often in the opposite direction to those in the UK. It is also interesting to note that Sheppard found that changes in the currency ratio were relatively more important than changes in the reserve ratio in influencing changes in the UK money supply (particularly after 1948). In contrast, changes in the reserve ratio had a greater impact on changes in the US money supply than did changes in the currency ratio (particularly after 1932).

Cagan (1965) also studied the determinants of the changes of the US money supply between 1875 and 1960. During the period 1875–1955 the money supply (defined as currency held outside the banking sector plus all deposits at commercial banks) grew at an annual rate of nearly 6 per cent and Cagan found that 90 per cent of this secular growth could be attributed to the expansion of high-powered money. The remaining 10 per cent was due to a decline in both the reserve ratio and the currency ratio.

While the growth of high-powered money dominated the long-term trend in the growth of the money supply, Cagan found that reserve and currency ratios played a more important role in cyclical changes in the money stock. During business expansions both ratios were generally found to fall, while in business contractions they were found to rise, thereby contributing to changes in the rate of growth of the money supply. Identifying eighteen cycles in the rate of growth of the money supply between 1877 and 1954, corresponding to business cycles, he found that the currency ratio was the proximate source of half the variation in the rate of monetary growth, with the reserve ratio and high-powered money each being responsible for about a quarter.

In the following sections we will discuss a number of criticisms that have been levied against the methodology of the monetary base approach. These criticisms relate in particular to the assumptions underlying the analysis and to the way in which the money supply process and its generation are conceived to operate.

3.3 The monetary base approach and the New View

3.3.1 *A mechanistic approach?*

The studies referred to in the previous section showed that there was considerable variation in the relative importance of these determinants within the various sub-periods. Hence it is apparent that changes in both asset preference ratios must be capable of accurate estimation and prediction if the model is to be used to predict changes in the money supply following changes in the monetary base. In this connection, J. Tobin (1965) has argued that it is purely arithmetic tautology to express the stock of money in terms of the volume of high-powered money, the reserve and currency ratios, and to explain its development over time by variations in these proximate determinants. The criticism that the monetary base approach is mechanistic and tautologous has however been denied by monetarists.

Monetarists argue that both the reserve and currency ratios are not taken as constants but are viewed as being behavioural parameters. The values of both ratios can be taken as constant only by assuming that the variables affecting them remain unchanged (i.e. the *ceteris paribus* assumption). They contend that both ratios will, for example, depend upon and vary inversely with the rate of interest. The banks' reserve ratio (ρ) reflects not only legally fixed reserve requirements but also reserves held as a voluntary precaution against unexpected deposit withdrawals by the public. As a result, a gap may exist between the minimum legally required and the observed ratios maintained by the banks. If there are unexpected withdrawals of deposits and the banks are not holding excess reserves, then they would have to sell their income-earning assets quickly, possibly incurring capital losses. The opportunity cost of holding excess reserves instead of income-earning assets is the rate of interest. Consequently, the reserve ratio will vary inversely with the rate of interest.

The rate of interest will also influence the fraction of deposits held by the public in the form of notes and coins. If the rate of interest increases, then *ceteris paribus*, the currency ratio will fall as the inducement to hold bank deposits increases at the expense of currency holdings. The money supply will, as a result, be positively related to the rate of interest, as both ratios are inverse functions of the rate of interest, and if either ratio falls the money supply will increase. We now have

$$M = \frac{1 + \lambda(r)}{\rho(r) + \lambda(r)} H. \tag{3.10}$$

In discussing the money supply function there is one final complication that needs to be taken into account, namely the existence of the discounting privilege. This privilege allows banks to sell certain classes of assets to the central bank, at a discount, should they need to replenish reserves quickly. The existence of this practice therefore reduces the demand for excess reserves by allowing easy bond sales. If the discount rate is increased, this facility will become less attractive for banks to use. As a result borrowed reserves of high-powered money will vary inversely with the discount rate.

The money supply can be expressed then as a function of the supply of high-powered money (H), the rate of interest (r), and the discount rate (R):

$$M = f(H, r, R). \tag{3.11}$$

Although the rate of interest will influence the currency and reserve ratios and hence the money supply, it is assumed that the monetary authorities can control the money supply by determining the supply of high-powered money and the discount rate.

3.3.2 *The New View*

The monetary base approach has been strongly criticised by adherents of the New View of money. The New View has been developed by academics at Yale University under the leadership of J. Tobin. In his essay, 'Commercial Banks as Creators of Money', Tobin (1963) outlined what he called the Old View of money in which commercial banks are sharply distinguished from other financial intermediaries. As commercial bank liabilities (deposits) serve as a means of payment, banks have traditionally been considered unique because they are the only financial intermediary that can create money. Consequently, they have to be restrained in their expansion of deposits by the imposition of reserve requirements. In contrast, non-bank financial intermediaries have traditionally been considered as being able only to transmit as opposed to being able to create credit. They cannot make loans by creating deposits, for unlike banks they cannot count on receiving back the deposit if they increase their lending. Before a non-bank financial intermediary can make a loan, therefore, it must attract a corresponding deposit. In the Old View the basis of the distinction between banks and non-bank financial intermediaries is that, unlike those of banks, the liabilities of non-bank financial intermediaries are not generally accepted as a means of payment and are, therefore, not money.

These distinctions between commercial banks and other financial intermediaries, and between money and other assets (sharply drawn in the old view), is blurred in the new view. Proponents of the new view have adopted the approach that monetary theory is the theory of portfolio management by economic units (households, firms, financial intermediaries and the government). The view that the money supply is an autonomous variable controlled by the government, implicit within the monetary base approach, has been criticised by adherents of the New View, who regard the money supply as an endogenous variable reflecting the behaviour of banks and other economic units. Rather than concentrating on the quantity of money and its velocity, attention is focused on the demand for and supply of a whole spectrum of assets, asset yields and the availability of credit.

Proponents of the New View deny that banks can always expand loans and deposits subject only to the constraint of meeting reserve requirements. Banks, it is argued, are like all financial intermediaries in that they can lend only to the extent to which the public is prepared to make deposits with them. The size of deposits will be determined by depositors' preferences, which will in turn be related to the rate of interest paid on such deposits and other pecuniary or non-pecuniary advantages of holding bank deposits. The size of banks' assets will be determined by the lending and financial/ investment opportunities available to the banks. It is held that the multiple creation of deposits, put forward in the Old View, will in fact run dry when the marginal revenue gained by making one more loan is less than the marginal cost of attracting and holding one more deposit (defined as the increase in total interest payments, on both existing and additional deposits, incurred by the bank in securing the additional deposit). This process, it is contended, will limit the size of all financial intermediaries, so that for all financial intermediaries including banks, borrowing and lending in a free market will be extended up to the point where marginal revenue equals marginal cost. It is argued that for banks the imposition of reserve requirements has cut off the process of expansion at a point where marginal revenue is greater than marginal cost, so that on acquiring additional reserves they can expand credit and deposits. The special place traditionally attributed to banks among financial intermediaries is seen, in the New View, to be due to the reserve requirements and interest rate ceilings to which banks have been subjected.

The origin of the New View can be found in the writings of Gurley and Shaw. In examining the financial aspects of economic development they have argued that banks are only one among many different types of financial intermediary that have shared in the function of facilitating the provision of finance by transmitting credit from ultimate lenders (surplus units) to ultimate borrowers (deficit units). As well as having played an important role in the provision of finance for development, both banks and non-bank financial intermediaries have created credit and increased the total flow of credit. Consequently Gurley and Shaw have advocated that financial, rather than solely monetary, control is needed to increase the effectiveness of monetary policy in influencing the economy.

3.3.3   *The monetarist response*

In response to the criticism made by proponents of the New View that the money supply is an endogenous variable reflecting the behaviour of banks and other economic units, monetarists agree that both the commercial banks and the public can affect the supply of money. Although the authorities will no longer have complete control over the money supply by altering the volume of high-powered money where the reserve and currency ratios are not constant, monetarists argue that this does not necessitate the abandonment of the monetary base approach. They maintain that the central bank has the ability to dominate the behaviour of the banks and the public and can offset the effects of changes in the reserve and currency ratios on the money supply, if the authorities choose to make the control of the money supply the target of their policies.

The monetary base approach and the New View can be reconciled in practice, if not in theory, provided the legal reserve ratio requirement imposed on the banks is greater than the ratio they would have chosen for themselves. In this case expansion of bank deposits, until marginal cost equals marginal revenue, will be arbitrarily prevented by the reserve ratio requirement; and therefore the multiple expansion of bank deposits, in response to the acquisition of extra reserve assets, is consistent with the New View.

3.4 The determination of the monetary base

A major criticism made against the monetary base approach relates to the critical assumption made in the analysis that the volume of high-powered money is exogenously determined by the monetary authorities. It is, therefore, necessary to examine the factors that determine the stock of high-powered money and the ways in which high-powered money is created, and to do this we will now discuss the provision of finance to the public sector.

3.4.1 *The determinants of the stock of high-powered money*

The public sector will be in deficit when its expenditure is greater than its revenue. A public sector deficit (PSD) can be financed by borrowing from other sectors in the following ways:
(1) net open market sales of government debt to the public (OMO) (net sales are defined as total open market sales minus finance required to pay off maturing government debt);
(2) sales of non-marketable debt (NMD), e.g. national savings;
(3) balance of payments flows (BPF – the combined current and

capital accounts), i.e. finance arising from balance of payments deficits (discussed more fully below);
(4) increases in the public sector's monetary liabilities.

This final form of public sector borrowing results in an increase in high-powered money ($\triangle H$). Hence

$$PSD \equiv OMO + NMD + BPF + \triangle H. \tag{3.12}$$

(The definition of these terms in the context of the UK financial system is incorporated in appendix 1 to this chapter.) If we assume that changes in high-powered money is the residual method of financing the public sector deficit and that high-powered money can be created only by the government, the above accounting identity can be rearranged to define changes in high-powered money as:

$$\Delta H \equiv PSD - OMO - NMD - BPF. \tag{3.13}$$

Control of the money supply, given the size of the public sector deficit, thus entails control of changes in high-powered money through control of the other three items on the right-hand side of the above identity (3.13). However, in a situation where the authorities have other targets, apart from control of the money supply, they may not be able to control the volume of high-powered money and, therefore, the money supply independently. Under certain circumstances the volume of high-powered money and the money supply may become endogenous.

3.4.2 *Endogeneity of high-powered money: fixed exchange rates*

One situation where high-powered money becomes endogenous is with a regime of fixed exchange rates. Under fixed exchange rates the price of the domestic currency in terms of the foreign currency is fixed and can be altered only by government decisions either to devalue or revalue the currency. The monetary authorities are therefore committed to buy and sell foreign exchange for the home currency at a fixed price. In the UK the foreign exchange account (known as the Exchange Equalisation Account) is managed by the Bank of England on behalf of the government. In the case of a balance of payments deficit, residents who require foreign exchange will buy it from the foreign exchange account with home currency.

Thus the balance of payments deficit provides additional finance to the authorities so that, in terms of the identity (3.13), this flow is a deduction from the public sector deficit. Given the size of the other components on the right-hand side of the identity, *ceteris paribus*, a balance of payments deficit must lead to a decrease in high-powered money and, therefore, ultimately the money supply. Conversely, in the case of a balance of payment surplus, residents will sell foreign exchange for the home currency, and the authorities will therefore have to raise additional finance, so that *ceteris paribus*, high-powered money will increase. The authorities may attempt to neutralise the effect of balance of payments deficits/surpluses on the volume of high-powered money by buying/selling bonds from/to the public and/or increasing/reducing the size of the public sector deficit. In other words, the authorities would try to bring about changes identical in magnitude, but opposite in sign, in the remaining components of the right-hand side of the identity (3.13), thus exactly offsetting the change in balance of payments flows. Monetarists however argue that the authorities cannot sterilise balance of payments deficits/surpluses for any significant period of time (see chapter 7). The above discussion has taken place within the context of a regime of fixed exchange rates, but the same effects would take place in a regime of managed flexibility to the extent that the authorities fixed and supported the exchange rate.

A balance of payments deficit will tend to decrease the money supply, or its rate of growth, and vice versa. As a result the concept of domestic credit expansion has been developed to take account of any reduction in the money supply resulting from a balance of payments deficit or increase resulting from a surplus. Domestic credit expansion is equal to approximately the increase in the domestic money supply plus any deficit on the balance of payments, or the increase in the domestic money supply minus any surplus on the balance of payments. It is therefore useful as an indication of how far monetary expansion is the result of domestic forces. The rate of growth of the money supply ($\dot{M}$) will then equal by definition the rate of change of foreign exchange reserves ($\dot{R}$), reflecting the balance of payments position, plus the rate of growth of the domestic money supply ($\dot{D}$, i.e. domestic credit expansion), so that for an open economy operating under fixed exchange rates,

$$\dot{M} = \dot{R} + \dot{D}. \tag{3.14}$$

On the other hand, in a regime of pure floating exchange rates, the exchange rate adjusts to clear the foreign exchange market so that the balance of payments is always zero and domestic credit expansion equals the rate of growth of the money supply.

3.4.3   *Endogeneity of high-powered money: stabilisation of interest rates*

The volume of high-powered money and the money supply will also become endogenous where the authorities pursue a policy of stabilising interest rates. The authorities can control either the rate of interest, through fixing the price of bonds, or alternatively the quantity of bonds, but not both simultaneously. Thus if they wish to fix or stabilise the rate of interest, the authorities must ensure that the supply of bonds is equal to the quantity demanded by the market at that particular rate of interest. In other words, open market operations and, therefore, the volume of high-powered money and the money supply become endogenous. If, for example, incomes rise relative to money balances, people would be induced to sell financial assets to restore their liquidity. In order to stabilise interest rates the authorities will buy the financial assets (open market operations) with high-powered money. As a result, control over the money supply is lost and the money supply will become endogenous, tending to vary directly with money incomes. Conversely the authorities can fix the level of open market operations and, therefore, control the volume of high-powered money and the money supply, but in so doing they must allow the market to determine the rate of interest at which it is willing to hold the supply of government bonds consistent with the specified level of open market operations.

In terms of the $IS - LM$ framework, a horizontal LM curve will be traced out at the level of interest rates that the authorities choose to stabilise. This is illustrated in figure 3.5. Starting from the intersection of the curves IS_0 and LM_0, the rate of interest is r^*. If the authorities choose to stabilise the rate of interest at this level an expansionary impulse from the goods market would initially cause the interest rate to rise as the IS curve moves from IS_0 to IS_1, intersecting LM_0. However, by adopting an expansionary monetary policy, shown by the shift in the LM curve downwards and to the right from LM_0 to LM_1, the rate of interest can be stabilised at r^*.

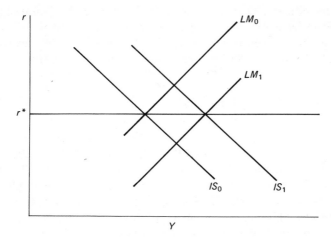

Figure 3.5

Likewise, an increase in the public sector deficit will, *ceteris paribus*, lead to an increase in the quantity of high-powered money. This particular case is likely to arise when the government is unwilling to allow the rate of interest to rise in response to the increase in the public sector deficit, so that again the level of open market operations, and therefore the quantity of high-powered money and the money supply, become endogenous.

Owing, therefore, to the pursuit of objectives other than control of the money supply, the authorities may allow the money supply to increase or decrease in response to changes in the demand for money. Monetarists accept that under such circumstances the money supply will become endogenous. Proponents of the monetary base approach, however, assume that the authorities can control the quantity of high-powered money if they choose to do so and that they can finance government expenditure without increasing the monetary base. Furthermore it is argued that, if the authorities do not do so, then they must be presumed to have chosen an expansion of the base.

3.4.4 *Policy implications*

What are the policy implications of the monetarist stance that the authorities can control the money supply if they choose to do so?

For an open economy wishing to operate an independent monetary policy, monetarists argue that it is essential to adopt a flexible, rather than a fixed, exchange rate system, so that balance of payments flows equal zero. Otherwise, under a fixed exchange rate regime a country will suffer from an inability to hold down the rate of growth of the money supply in the face of a balance of payments surplus. In anything other than a situation of clean floating, the money supply will be influenced by the balance of payments. Further, if the authorities wish to control the money supply, they must forsake policies of stabilising interest rates. In order to control the monetary base, interest rates would have to vary in order to bring about such changes in asset holdings and debt commitments as were necessary to permit the financing of the public sector deficit without expansion of the money supply. If the authorities wish to control and insulate the money supply from the public sector deficit, they must forsake control over interest rates.

3.5   Empirical evidence

In this final section we will review the empirical evidence put forward for the United States to support the monetarist belief that changes in the stock of money play a largely independent role in cyclical fluctuations.

3.5.1   *The timing of monetary changes*

The first kind of empirical evidence, although not providing the primary basis for the view, has caused the most criticism. This is the empirically observed tendency for monetary changes to precede changes in business activity (see chapter 5 for a discussion of this empirical evidence). Criticism has been made that timing evidence cannot be accepted as empirical proof of propositions about causation. What appears to be a positive relation with a lead may be an inverted relation with a lag, in that the lead may be simply a reflection of an earlier influence of business on money. Also, the monetary changes and business changes might be the result of some other influences which have their effect on money more promptly than on business activity. Monetarists, however, agree that the regular and sizable leads of the money supply are by no means decisive but argue that they are suggestive of an influence running from money to business. The conclusion of the importance of monetary changes is not based primarily on observed timing relations.

3.5.2 *Cyclical fluctuations*

The two additional strands of empirical evidence that provide the basic foundation to the belief in the largely independent role of money have come from the study of the monetary history of the United States between 1867 and 1960, undertaken by Friedman and Schwartz (1963b). In their study they found that the stock of money had tended to rise during both cyclical expansions and contractions. Cyclical behaviour showed up in different rates of growth of the money supply, rather than as an absolute rise or fall in the money stock, with a slower rate of growth of the money supply occurring during contractions than during expansions in the level of economic activity. However, the only times when there was an appreciable absolute fall in the money stock were also periods of severe economic contraction. Within the ninety-three-year period examined by Friedman and Schwartz six such periods can be identified: (1) 1873–79, (2) 1893–94, (3) 1907–08, (4) 1920–21, (5) 1929–33 and (6) 1937–38.

It is argued that all the major American recessions owe their severity to the events (financial and/or political) that produced an absolute contraction in the money supply. From the study of the historical circumstances underlying the changes that occurred in the money stock, it is argued that the factors producing the changes were mainly independent of contemporary or prior changes in nominal income and prices, and could be generally attributed to specific historical circumstances. For example, Friedman and Schwartz have argued that the absolute decline that took place in the money stock between both 1920–21 and 1937–38 was a consequence of highly restrictive policy actions undertaken by the Federal Reserve System (e.g., reserve requirements were doubled in 1936 and 1937). The policy actions undertaken were themselves quickly followed by sharp declines in the money stock, which were in turn followed by a period of severe economic contraction. In Friedman's and Schwartz's view the belief that monetary changes were a cause, rather than a consequence, of the associated period of economic contraction is also supported by the events surrounding the 1929–33 contraction. It had been widely interpreted in analysing the 1929–33 depression that monetary factors were not critical and that real factors were the key to the depression. The standard interpretation has been that it was impossible to use monetary policy either to offset the downturn or to promote an upturn once the trough had been reached. Friedman and Schwartz have argued that, in contrast, the downturn was a consequence of monetary change and that the lack of a sufficiently expansionary policy prolonged the trough. An initial mild decline in the money stock from 1929 to 1930 was converted into a sharp decline by a wave of bank failures beginning late in 1930. Those failures produced an increase in the public's demand for currency as a fraction of deposits (λ), owing to the loss of faith in the banks' ability to redeem deposits, and an increase in the banks' cash reserve ratio (ρ), owing to the banks' loss of faith in the public's willingness to maintain their deposits with them. The decline in the money stock consequent upon the rise in both ratios was further intensified by the restrictive action undertaken by the Federal Reserve in October 1931 in raising the discount rate. With the central bank failing to increase the quantity of high-powered money sufficiently to offset the rise in both ratios, the money stock fell by about a third between October 1929 and June 1933. By adopting alternative policies, it is contended that the Federal Reserve System could have kept the money stock from falling: e.g. by providing enough high-powered money to satisfy the banks' desire for liquidity owing to the increase in the currency ratio. Friedman and Schwartz argue that disturbances originating in the monetary sector were the cause of disturbances in the level of economic activity.

3.5.3   *The diversity of monetary experience*

The third piece of evidence justifying the belief that changes in the stock of money play a largely independent role in cyclical fluctuations is that for the United States, even under substantially different monetary arrangements that have existed over the period 1867–1960, the cyclical movements in money have had much the same relation (both in timing and amplitude) to cyclical movements in business activity. Based on the examination of major recessions, the belief is that money also plays an important role in most minor recessions.

3.5.4 *Concluding remarks*

Monetarists claim that the empirical evidence discussed above supports their view that the money supply has been exogenously determined during certain periods of American history and that, during these periods, changes in the money supply have caused changes in economic activity rather than the other way around. Friedman has argued that during other periods changes in the money stock were a consequence, as well as an independent source, of changes in nominal income and prices. It is argued that, once changes in the money stock occurred, they produced in their turn still further effects on income and prices (mutual interaction).

This does not mean however that money was the only factor that affected the course of economic activity. All too often monetarists are crudely branded as believing that money is all that matters, analogous to the equally crude branding of Keynesians believing that money does not matter at all.

Appendix 1 : The Application of the Monetary Base Model to the UK

The monetary base model analysed in this chapter needs modifications for application to the UK. In the UK the reserve base is composed of a variety of public and private short-term liabilities. The 12½ per cent reserve asset base, which applies to all banks is formed by:

(1) balances at the Bank of England, excluding special deposits;
(2) money at call and short notice (mainly to the discount houses);
(3) British government and Northern Ireland government Treasury bills;
(4) British government securities with less than a year to maturity;
(5) local authority bills;
(6) commercial bills of exchange, subject to the constraint that they shall not form more than 2 per cent of the 12½ per cent ratio.

Within this framework, the expansion of high-powered money following a public sector deficit needs amplification. In the context of the UK financial system, the residual form of finance is that derived from sales of Treasury bills to the banking sector (including discount houses). When banks purchase Treasury bills their balances at the Bank of England will be lowered but their holdings of reserve assets will remain constant because Treasury bills are reserve assets. If the purchase of Treasury bills is carried out by the discount houses, who obtain loans from the banks, then money at call or short notice will increase. So again, while the composition of reserve assets may have changed, the total remains constant. When the government carries out the expenditure for which the finance was raised, then the banks' balances at the Bank of England will return to their former level but this will leave the banks with extra reserve assets. The banks' balances at the Bank of England will remain unchanged but their holdings of either Treasury bills or money at call or at short notice will increase.

Thus within the context of the identity:

$$\Delta H \equiv PSD - OMO - NMD - BPF$$

where *OMO* refers to sales of securities other than the sales of Treasury bills (or other reserve assets) to the banking sector and ΔH includes all reserve assets sold to the banking sector as well as currency.

The interested reader will find a special issue of *The Manchester School* (vol. 41, March 1973), devoted to the competition and credit control regime, introduced in the United Kingdom in 1971. Particularly recommended for student reading is the article by E. V. Morgan and R. L. Harrington, entitled 'Reserve Assets and the Supply of Money', which examines the ability of the authorities to influence the money supply given the various assets that qualify as reserve assets for banks.

Bibliography

*Titles marked * are particularly recommended for student reading.*

*Artis, M. J. (1973), 'Analysis of the Determination of the Stock of Money: Discussion'. In *Essays in Modern Economics*, edited by M. Parkin and A. R. Nobay (London: Longman).

Bain, A. D. (1970), *The Control of the Money Supply*. (Harmondsworth: Penguin.)

Bank of England (1969), 'Domestic Credit Expansion'. *Bank of England Quarterly Bulletin*, vol. 9 (September).

Bank of England (1971), 'Competition and Credit Control'. *Bank of England Quarterly Bulletin*, vol. 11 (June).

Cagan, P. (1965), *Determinants and Effects of Changes in the Stock of Money, 1875–1960*. National Bureau of Economic Research Studies in Business Cycles, no. 13. (New York: Columbia University Press.)

Davidson, P. and Weintraub, S. (1973), 'Money as Cause and Effect'. *Economic Journal*, vol. 83 (December).

*Friedman, M. (1958), 'The Supply of Money and Changes in Prices and Output'. Reprinted in the *Optimum Quantity of Money and Other Essays* (Chicago: Aldine, 1969).

*Friedman, M. (1970), 'The New Monetarism: Comment'. *Lloyds Bank Review*, no. 98 (October).

*Friedman, M. and Schwartz, A. J. (1963a), 'Money and Business Cycles'. *Review of Economics and Statistics*, vol. 45, part 2 supplement (February).

Reprinted in *The Optimum Quantity of Money and Other Essays* (Chicago: Aldine, 1969).

Friedman, M. and Schwartz, A. J. (1963b), *A Monetary History of the United States, 1867–1960*. National Bureau of Economic Research Studies in Business Cycles, no. 12 (Princeton: University Press).

Friedman, M. and Schwartz, A. J. (1969), 'The Definition of Money: Net Wealth and Neutrality as Criteria'. *Journal of Money, Credit, and Banking*, vol. 1 (February).

Friedman, M. and Schwartz, A. J. (1970), *Monetary Statistics of the United States*. National Bureau of Economic Research Studies in Business Cycles, no. 20 (New York: Columbia University Press).

*Goodhart, C. A. E. (1973), 'Analysis of the Determination of the Stock of Money'. In *Essays in Modern Economics*, edited by M. Parkin and A. R. Nobay (London: Longman).

Gurley, J. G. and Shaw, E. S. (1955), 'Financial Aspects of Economic Developmen'. *American Economic Review*, vol. 45 (September).

Gurley, J. G. and Shaw, E. S. (1956), 'Financial Intermediaries and the Saving-Investment Process'. *Journal of Finance*, vol. 11 (May).

Gurley, J. G. and Shaw, E. S. (1960), *Money in a Theory of Finance*. (Washington: The Brookings Institution.)

*Kaldor, N. (1970), 'The New Monetarism'. *Lloyds Bank Review*, no. 97 (July).

Laidler, D. (1969), 'The Definition of Money'. *Journal of Money, Credit and Banking*, vol. 1 (August).

Sheppard, D. K. (1971), *The Growth and Role of UK Financial Institutions 1880–1962* (Methuen: London).

Sims, C. A. (1972), 'Money, Finance, and Causality'. *American Economic Review*, vol. 62 (September).

*Tobin, J. (1963), 'Commercial Banks as Creators of Money'. In *Banking and Monetary Studies*, edited by D. Carson (Homewood, Illinois: Richard Irwin).

*Tobin, J (1965), 'The Monetary Interpretation of History'. *American Economic Review*, vol. 55 (June).

Tobin, J. (1970), 'Money and Income: Post Hoc Ergo Propter Hoc?' *Quarterly Journal of Economics*, vol. 84 (May).

Tobin, J. and Brainard, W. C. (1963), 'Financial Intermediaries and the Effectiveness of Monetary Controls'. *American Economic Review*, vol. 53 (May).

4 Money and Inflation

4.1 Inflation: the nature of the controversy

Inflation can be defined as a process of continually rising prices (i.e. the general price level, not just some prices) and is, therefore, equivalent by definition to a continually falling value of money. However, while inflation and monetary expansion have always occurred simultaneously, there is a considerable degree of controversy over the direction of causation. Some would argue that monetary expansion is the proximate cause of inflation, whereas others insist that monetary expansion is merely the response to an inflationary process caused by other (i.e. non-monetary) factors. Explanations of inflation can be classified into two broad groups, (1) sociological and (2) monetary. We wish to stress that, in order to facilitate the discussion of inflation, we are posing these two views as alternatives. It is, of course, perfectly possible to take a compromise or eclectic position that both sociological and monetary factors are important. In this case, the greater the importance attached to sociological as opposed to monetary factors, the more closely the eclectic stance approximates the sociological view. Conversely, where monetary factors are believed to be relatively more important, the more closely the eclectic stance approximates the monetarist viewpoint, which we will examine in detail in the rest of this chapter.

In the sociological explanation, wage increases are regarded as the initiating force of inflation. It is argued that these wage increases can occur independently of demand and supply conditions in the labour market because of, for example, the actions of trade union leaders (Wiles, 1973); a decline in the general moral climate (Wiles, 1973; Harrod, 1972); inconsistent views of a fair wage structure (Hicks, 1975) and government guarantees of full employment (Phelps-Brown, 1975). There exists, therefore, a wide divergence of views as to what kinds of social pressure cause the rise in money wages. Given these pressures, the common strand within the sociological approach is that wages are an important component of the total cost of production and, if money wages continually rise faster than the growth of productivity, then inflation will result. In the absence of monetary expansion, inflation will reduce the real value of the money supply and will result in higher unemployment. In order to maintain full employment (however defined), the government will increase the money supply. This response by the government explains the high degree of correlation between money changes and price increases, but in the sociological view causation runs from price increases to changes in the money supply. The crucial conclusion from these arguments is that, whatever may be true in the past, the present inflation is not amenable to control by orthodox monetary contraction. This would merely raise the level of unemployment but would not reduce the rate of inflation (at least not significantly) within the confines of politically feasible levels of unemployment.

Monetarists, on the other hand, contend that the origins of inflation are always excessive monetary expansion by the authorities and that this leads to excess demand in the labour and product markets, thus initiating an inflationary process. Monetarists would then accept the dictum put forward by Friedman (1970) that: 'Inflation is always and everywhere a monetary phenomenon in the sense that it is and can be produced only by a more rapid increase in the quantity of money than in output.' Monetarists do recognise that socio-political factors have a role to play in the analysis of inflation. They argue, however, that these factors influence the behaviour of the government and, therefore, the rate of monetary expansion rather than directly influencing the rate of inflation. Hence, in contrast to the sociological viewpoint, the actions of trade unions affect only the transition or adjustment paths of the economy and not the final level of inflation. In other words, once the rate of monetary expansion is determined, so, in the long run, is the rate of inflation.

The distinction between these approaches is illustrated in figure 4.1 (which omits, for ease of exposition, the role played by expectations).

In this chapter we shall examine in more detail the monetarist theory of inflation, starting from the quantity theory predictions

(1) Sociological view

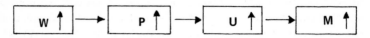

(2) Monetarist view

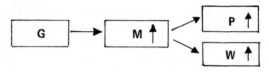

Figure 4.1

(section 4.2) before examining, within this theory, the roles of the basic and the expectations – augmented Phillips curves in sections 4.3 and 4.4. This will lead to a consideration of the natural rate of unemployment in section 4.5. The distinction between real and nominal rates of interest will also be considered (section 4.6), and finally the analysis will be extended to the open economy in section 4.7.

4.2   Inflation and the quantity theory

4.2.1   *The traditional quantity theory*

In chapter 2 we discussed the traditional quantity theory of money, which postulated a purely monetary explanation of the determination of the general price level. Any increase in the money supply would, it was argued, lead to a proportionate increase in the general price level, while a continuous expansion of the money supply would lead to a continuous rise in the price level (i.e. inflation). This can easily be demonstrated by referring to the formulation of the quantity theory discussed in section 1.2.1:

$$MV = PO \tag{4.1}$$

Using the standard assumptions that O and V are constant and M is exogenous, (4.1) can be rearranged to

$$P = \alpha M \tag{4.2}$$

where $\alpha = V/O$. Differentiating (4.2) with respect to time and dividing throughout so as to obtain proportionate rates of change gives the standard quantity theory prediction that the rate of inflation equals the proportionate rate of growth of the money supply:

$$\dot{P} = \dot{M} \tag{4.3}$$

If the assumption that output is constant is relaxed, equation (4.3) becomes

$$\dot{P} = \dot{M} - \dot{O} \tag{4.4}$$

i.e. the rate of inflation is equal to the rate of monetary expansion less the rate of growth of output.

As was explained in chapter 2, the growth of output was assumed to be a function of real factors only, and therefore to be independent of the rate of monetary expansion. Also in chapter 2, we discussed the other assumptions underlying this analysis, namely that the demand for and supply of money were determined independently of each other, and that the factors affecting the demand for real balances changed slowly over time, if at all. As a result of these assumptions, the determination of the general price level and its rate of change (i.e. inflation) was analysed by considering equilibrium, and the effect on that equilibrium of changes in the money supply within the money market. A partial equilibrium analysis was thus employed.

4.2.2 *The modern quantity theory*

In the modern quantity theory, the independence of the demand for and supply of money is destroyed by the introduction of the expected rate of inflation into the demand for money function. As we shall discuss more fully later, monetarists argue that an increase in the rate of monetary expansion will lead to an increase in the actual rate of inflation. This increase in the actual rate of inflation would cause individuals to revise upwards their expectations of future rates of inflation, which, it is argued, would reduce the real quantity of money demanded. Given the predicted inverse relationship between the demand for real balances and the rate of inflation, the interesting question arises as to whether the inflationary process would be dynamically stable. In other words, could an increase in the money supply lead to a situation where the ensuing inflation lowered the demand for money to such an extent (a flight from money) that hyper-inflation resulted? This possibility is more likely, (a) the greater the elasticity of the demand for money with respect to the expected rate of inflation and (b) the greater the elasticity of the expected rate with respect to the actual rate of inflation. The results from a number of studies (for example the study of seven European hyper-inflations by Cagan, 1956) have suggested that both elasticities are not large enough to lead to a flight from money and, therefore, to a self-generating inflation.

This recognition of the interdependence between the demand for and supply of money is only one aspect of the difference between the modern quantity theory and the traditional theory. As we have seen earlier in this section, the use of partial equilibrium analysis within the quantity theory approach depends critically on the assumed independence in the long run of the growth of real output ($\dot{O}$ in equation 4.4) and the rate of monetary expansion. If, however, monetary expansion does influence the rate of growth of real output, it is not possible to analyse inflation without considering the goods and labour markets in addition to the money markets and, of course, the interaction between all three of these markets. Laidler and Parkin (1975) have concluded that the almost universal result, despite a wide range of assumptions, in the economic growth literature is that money is not neutral; i.e., it influences real income and output in the long run. (See, for example, Parkin, 1977, for a discussion of the ways in which inflation, even if fully anticipated, may affect the rate of economic growth.) Thus modern monetarist analysis suggests that partial equilibrium analysis of inflation is inadequate and that a complete model of the economy is necessary to carry out analysis of inflation. Therefore in our discussion of monetarist views on the nature of the inflationary process, it is necessary to examine the labour market with particular reference to the nature and development of the Phillips curve analysis.

4.3   The Phillips curve

4.3.1   *Origins of the analysis*

In general terms this analysis is concerned with the relationship between the level of excess demand for labour and the rate of change of money wages. In order to link changes in money wages to changes in the price level, it is commonly assumed that the rate of change of prices (i.e. the rate of inflation) is equal to the rate of change of money wages less the rate of growth of productivity. This formulation takes for granted that there is no change in the share of labour in national income. Obviously wages can rise without prices rising if it is just a case of the transfer of income from profits to wages. We shall use the assumption of constant shares in national income throughout the rest of the chapter.

The main development of this analysis commenced with the examination by Phillips (1958) of the statistical relationship between unemployment and the rate of change of money wages over the period 1861 – 1957. For the period 1861 – 1913, Phillips was able to estimate an inverse relationship between unemployment (U) and the rate of change of money wages ($\dot{W}$), which could predict accurately the relationship between the two variables for the period 1951–57. The estimated average relationship was nonlinear and appeared to show that, at an unemployment level of about $5\frac{1}{2}$ per cent, the rate of change of money wages was zero. Furthermore, at an unemployment level of approximately $2\frac{1}{2}$ per cent, the rate of change of money wages was approximately equal to the then-average growth of productivity in Britain (i.e. 2 per cent), so that

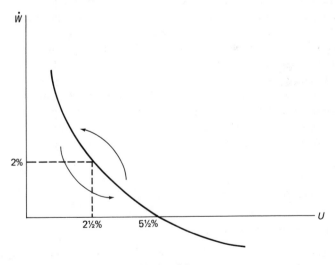

Figure 4.2

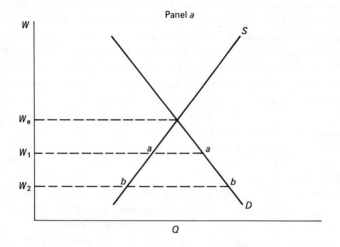

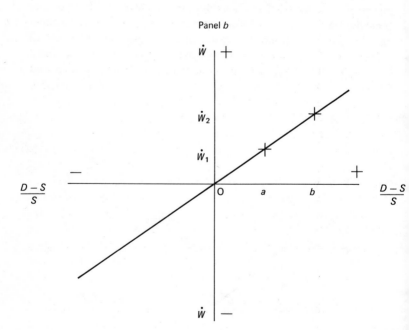

Figure 4.3

such wage rises were compatible with stable prices. An additional characteristic of the relationship was that, at least before 1939, the observed values of the rate of change of money wages lay above the average relationship when unemployment was falling and below the average relationship when unemployment was rising. This generated anti-clockwise loops around the average relationship. The general form of the function is shown in figure 4.2.

4.3.2 *Further development of the analysis*

This relationship was further examined by Lipsey (1960), who provided a more rigorous theoretical justification for the curve. Lipsey argued that, within a single market, the speed at which wages rise (or fall) will depend linearly on the degree of excess demand for labour in that market. This is illustrated in figure 4.3. Panel a uses standard demand and supply analysis. At any wage rate below W_e there is excess demand for labour. Thus at wage rate W_1 there is an excess demand for labour of aa (equal to Oa in panel b), and at W_2 an excess demand of bb (equal to Ob in panel b). Lipsey argued that wages would rise in conditions of excess demand for labour, and that the rate of increase in money wage rates would be faster, the larger the excess demand for labour. This relationship in linear form is depicted in panel b, where the excess demand for labour is specified in percentage form (i.e. $(D—S)/S$). The problem for quantification of this function was that the excess demand for labour could not be measured directly, and it was therefore necessary to use a proxy, or surrogate, for excess demand, e.g. the published unemployment statistics. In this connection it is important to realise that a zero excess demand (i.e. at wage rate W_e in figure 4.3 panel a) does not mean that registered unemployment will also be zero, but rather that there are jobs available for those willing to work at the ruling wage rate. At any point of time, individuals will be changing jobs and searching for new employment, and they will register as unemployed in order to obtain the social welfare benefits due to them.

Lipsey further argued that the relationship between excess demand and unemployment would be nonlinear because, although registered unemployment would fall in response to positive excess demand as jobs became easier to find, registered unemployment would only

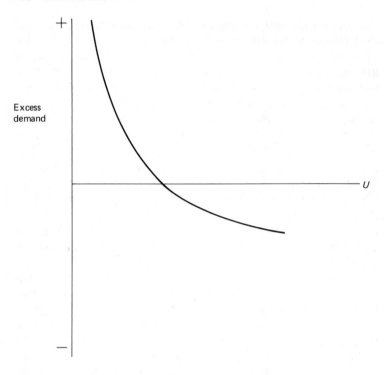

Figure 4.4

asymptotically approach zero. Lipsey thus postulated that a steadily increasing excess demand would be reflected in increasingly smaller reductions in unemployment. The relationship postulated between unemployment and excess demand is shown in figure 4.4.

The rationale for the nonlinear negative relationship between the rate of increase in money wages and registered unemployment was provided through the combination of (a) the positive linear relationship between the rate of increase in money wages and excess demand and (b) the negative nonlinear relationship between excess demand and unemployment. Therefore, the relationship between the rate of increase of money wages and unemployment in the individual market will conform to the general picture shown in figure 4.2, with a positive amount of frictional or search unemployment required for a zero growth in money wages. Aggregation over all markets will produce the macro Phillips curve.

Lipsey (1960) used the aggregation process to explain the anti-clockwise loops around the average relationship. Assume, for ease of exposition, that two equal size markets have identical micro-Phillips curves and unemployment falls in one market and not in the other (or more generally falls faster in one market than the other); then the rate of increase in money wages would be higher than that predicted by the individual micro-Phillips curves. This is demonstrated in figure 4.5. PC_m is the micro-Phillips curve. Unemployment is originally equal to Oa in both markets but falls to Ob in one market while remaining at Oa in the other market. The average rate of wage increase is equal to $OY[(OZ+O)/2]$, whereas the Phillips curve predicts that, for an average level of unemployment equal to $Od[(Ob+Oa)/2]$, the rate of wage increase should be OX. Thus Lipsey rationalised the existence of anti-clockwise loops around the average relationship on the grounds that, as the economy expanded, the fall in unemployment in the individual markets would be unequal with some markets experiencing faster expansion than others. Thus the average rate of wage increase across all markets would be higher than that predicted by the Phillips curve. In contrast, he postulated that during the downswing the rates of contraction would be roughly the same in all markets.

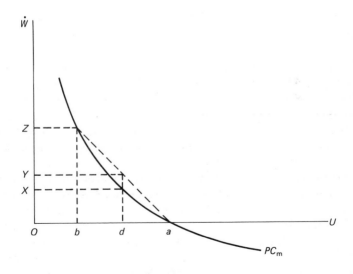

Figure 4.5

This completes the review of the basic Phillips curve and it only remains necessary to mention two additional points. First, the analysis is neutral as to whether the cause of inflation is a supply or a demand change in the labour market (i.e. cost-push or demand-pull) because (as reference to figure 4.3 panel *a* will show) excess demand at the ruling wage rate (W_e) could be caused by either an outward shift in the demand curve or a backward shift in the supply curve or both. Second, if the relationship between the rate of change of money wages and unemployment is observed to break down, this may be due to a breakdown in the relationships between either (a) the rate of change of money wages and excess demand for labour because it is incorrectly specified, or (b) excess demand for labour and unemployment.

4.3.3 *Criticisms of the analysis*

There are major problems associated with the above analysis of the Phillips curve. At the empirical level it was noticed that, post-1945, the loops were observed to operate in a clockwise direction (i.e. the opposite direction to the prewar experience). In addition, the whole relationship seemed to break down after 1967, when many countries experienced the simultaneous occurrence of rising unemployment and rising rates of inflation. Existing Phillips curve theory was unable to explain these two features. At the theoretical level, however, while the Phillips curve was concerned with the behaviour of money wages, orthodox microeconomic theory of the labour market suggested that the demand for and supply of labour should be specified in terms of real not money wages. Furthermore, since wage bargains are negotiated for discrete periods, both employers and employees can be expected to take into consideration not only the current price level in determining the real wage being negotiated, but also the rate of inflation expected to exist throughout the period of the contract. As a result the Phillips curve analysis has been augmented by the introduction of the expected rate of inflation as an additional variable determining the rate of change of money wages.

4.4   The expectations – augmented Phillips curve

4.4.1   *Formation of expectations*

Before we discuss the analysis, we must digress initially to discuss how expectations of future rates of inflation may be proxied by data that are directly observable. Within the literature two methods have generally been used, (1) adaptive and (2) rational expectations. At this stage we shall only describe briefly these two methods but the interested reader will find a more detailed examination in the appendix to this chapter.

Adaptive expectations arise when an individual, having learnt from past experience, revises his future expectations according to the divergence between the expected and actual values of the variable concerned. More formally, adaptive expectations implies that expectations of future rates of inflation are revised in each period proportionately (though less than completely) according to the gap between the realised or actual rate of inflation for a particular period and the value it was previously expected to attain in that period. This can be shown (see the appendix to this chapter) to be equivalent to the situation where an individual derives his views as to the values a variable is likely to attain, as a weighted average of the values that variable took in the past, with the weights declining geometrically over time.

The rational expectations hypothesis is based on the assumption that the individuals forming the expectations are rational and that expectations are based on the predictions of economic theory. Thus, for example, an individual who believed that inflation was a monetary phenomenon would derive his expectations as to the future rate of inflation according to the rate of monetary expansion, after incorporating the required lags.

As an alternative to specifying the way in which expectations are formed, there is also the method of measuring directly the expected values of inflation by survey techniques, the main example of this being the study by Carlson and Parkin (1975).

4.4.2   *Expectations and the Phillips curve*

By introducing the expected rate of inflation, while still maintaining the axes of the rate of increase of money wages ($\dot{W}$) and unemployment (U), we should expect to find not one unique macro Phillips

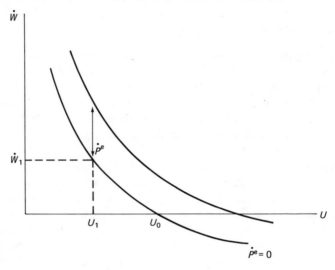

Figure 4.6

curve but instead a whole family of such curves with one curve for each expected rate of inflation. Indeed, as the expected rate of inflation increases, so the Phillips curve would shift upwards. This is illustrated diagrammatically in figure 4.6. For simplicity we will make the assumption that the growth of productivity remains constant at zero.

Equilibrium occurs initially at U_0 with a zero rate of wage increase so that, with the assumption of zero growth in productivity, the price level would be constant and the expected rate of inflation ($\dot{P}^e$) would be zero. If the government expanded aggregate demand so that unemployment fell to say U_1, then the rate of wage increase would rise to $\dot{W}_1$ and prices would increase by the rate of increase of money wages (i.e. $\dot{W}_1$). If price expectations are formed according to the adaptive expectations hypothesis, then sooner or later individuals and firms would start to expect future price increases and would take their expectations into consideration when entering into wage negotiations. This means that, if a real rate of wage increase of $\dot{W}_1$ is required, money wages would have to rise at a rate of $\dot{W}_1$ plus the expected rate of inflation; in other words, the

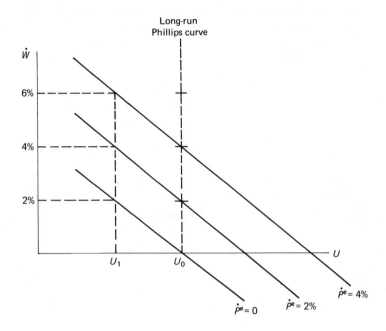

Figure 4.7

short-run Phillips curve would shift upwards. The crucial question is, how far does it shift? If the actual rate of inflation is completely anticipated in wage bargains, then the gap between the two curves in figure 4.6 will equal $\dot{W}_1 = \dot{P}^e$.

Complete anticipation of actual inflation is illustrated in figure 4.7, where for ease of diagrammatic presentation the Phillips curves are assumed to be linear. For example, at U_0, the rate of increase of money wages and the expected rate of inflation both equal zero. If the government reduced unemployment to U_1 by monetary expansion, then the rate of increase in money wages would be 2 per cent. Maintaining the assumption of no growth in productivity, a 2 per cent increase in the rate of wage inflation would lead to a 2 per cent rate of price inflation. If the rate of price inflation is fully anticipated by employers and employees, money wage rates would have to increase by 4 per cent to maintain the 2 per cent rise in real wages required by the continued existence of excess demand in the labour market. Similarly, in the following period prices would rise by 4 per cent, so money wages would have to rise by 6 per cent to attain the necessary 2 per cent increase in real wages. The Phillips curve would then shift upwards, and in order to maintain unemployment at U_1, the government would have to accept accelerating rates of inflation, e.g. in terms of figure 4.7, 2 per cent, then 4 per cent and then 6 per cent and so on. In contrast, if the rate of monetary expansion was not further increased, the rising price level would reduce the real value of the money supply. Unemployment would rise until such time as, in equilibrium, the rate of expansion of the money supply exactly equalled the percentage increase in the actual and expected rates of inflation, and unemployment would have returned to U_0. If all such points of the equilibrium are joined, we obtain the long-run Phillips curve which is vertical in the case where actual inflation is completely anticipated.

In order to maintain unemployment levels less than U_0, the authorities would have to increase continuously the rate of monetary expansion and therefore accept a continuously rising rate of inflation. On the other hand, at U_0 the rate of increase in money wages is exactly equalled by the rate of increase in prices, so that the real wage is constant, with the result that there would be no disturbance in the labour market. Similarly, the real value of the money supply would also remain constant, so that there would be no disturbance in the money market. U_0 has been termed the natural rate of unemployment (Friedman, 1968) and is the only level of unemployment at which a constant rate of inflation may be maintained. This analysis suggests that, to maintain unemployment below the natural rate, real wages must be kept below their equilibrium level. In order to do this, prices would have to rise at a faster rate than money wages, but in this case employees would revise upwards their expectations of inflation and press for higher wage increases, so that the end result would be an accelerating rate of wage increase (i.e. from 2 per cent to 4 per cent to 6 per cent etc.).

Mathematically the expectations-augmented Phillips curve can be expressed by the equation

$$\dot{W} = f(U) + \beta \dot{P}^e \tag{4.5}$$

The monetarist view is that in the long run $\beta = 1$, so that the rate of money wage increase is equal to a component determined by the state of excess demand plus the expected rate of inflation. If there is no excess demand, then the rate of increase of money wages would equal the expected rate of inflation, and only in the special case

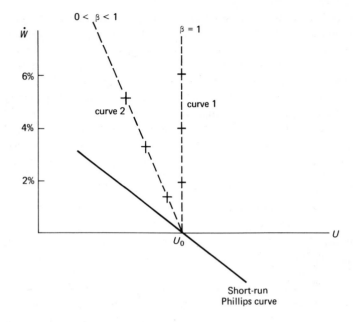

Figure 4.8

where the expected rate of inflation is zero would wage inflation be zero. Inflation is held by monetarists to be caused by excess demand, owing primarily to excessive monetary expansion and expectations regarding future rates of inflation.

This analysis predicts that there will be no long-run trade-off between unemployment and inflation but only a short-term benefit achieved at the expense of faster inflation later (as illustrated in figure 4.7). This, of course, depends on inflation being fully anticipated. If the individual economic units do not fully anticipate the rate of inflation in their negotiations, the short-run Phillips curve in figure 4.7 would not shift up by the full amount of the actual rate of inflation. The coefficient β in equation (4.5) would then be less than 1, with the result that the slope of the long-run Phillips curve would be steeper than that of the short-run curve but less than vertical. In this case, there would be a permanent trade-off between inflation and unemployment, but a less favourable one than that predicted by movement along the short-run Phillips curve. This is illustrated in figure 4.8. Curves 1 and 2 are long-run Phillips curves with $\beta = 1$ and with $\beta < 1$ respectively. Curve 1 is the vertical long-run Phillips curve with the same equilibrium points as those discussed for figure 4.7. Curve 2 shows the situation where β is less than 1 (i.e. inflation is not completely anticipated), so that it is possible to lower unemployment below the natural rate (U_0), but only at the cost of a higher rate of wage inflation $(\dot{W})$ than that predicted by the short-run Phillips curve. It is worth noting that if $\beta = O$, the long-run and the short-run Phillips curves would be the same.

4.4.3   *The augmented Phillips curve: an alternative rationale*

The above rationale of the augmented Phillips curve follows the arguments put forward by Friedman (1975), but an alternative rationale has been put forward by Phelps (1968). Phelps has postulated that firms form expectations about the future growth rate of money wages. If the individual firm is content with its level of employment, then it will raise its money wages by the same average percentage that it expects other firms to raise their wages. If it wants to increase the level of its employment because it is experiencing excess demand for its goods, it will increase money wages more than the expected average for other firms. Conversely, if it is experiencing deficient demand for its products and wishes to decrease employment, it will increase money wages at less than the average rate expected. Thus, on aggregation, the percentage change of money wages will be a function of the excess demand for labour plus the expected rate of change of money wages and, therefore, prices. The natural rate of unemployment is determined where the excess demand for labour by firms wishing to increase their employment is exactly matched by the excess supply of labour possessed by firms wishing to contract their labour force. In some respects this rationale of the augmented Phillips curve is more appealing since it provides a mechanism for firms to fix wages through wage offers, whereas the earlier rationale provides no such mechanism, just an assumption that excess demand will cause wage rates to rise through the interactions of demand and supply in the market.

Finally, in this section, we must emphasise that the Phelps formulation makes no difference at all to the predictions of the model. This formulation still predicts a long-run vertical Phillips curve so that there is no trade-off between inflation and unemployment in the long run. It is thought that it provides a more accurate description of how wages and prices are fixed in the real world.

4.4.4   *Empirical evidence*

The vital prediction of both the Phelps and Friedman formulation of the augmented Phillips curve hypothesis is that, for the equation

$$\dot{W} = f(U) + \beta \dot{P}^e \tag{4.5}$$

$\beta = 1$. It would be helpful if we could obtain econometric estimates of this equation and then test whether the estimated coefficient for β is significantly different from one. A word of caution is necessary here. Since there are no observed values for $\dot{P}^e$, any statistical test will always test two hypotheses simultaneously: first, that expectations are derived in the manner specified, and second, that $\beta = 1$. Unfortunately the empirical evidence is far from clear-cut and the issue of the possible existence of the long-run vertical Phillips curve is the subject of much controversy. For example, Solow (1969), using UK data, obtained an estimate for β of approximately 0.4. On the other hand Turnovsky (1972), using Canadian data, obtained a value of β not significantly different from 1, and similarly Saunders and Nobay (1972), using more sophisticated techniques to explain the formation of expectations, reported estimates of β roughly equal to 1 for UK data. Cross and Laidler (1975) reported the results of a study of price equations for twenty individual countries. There was no evidence of a long-run trade-off for any country. Cross and Laidler have argued that the failure of earlier studies to generate no long-run trade-off (i.e. a vertical long-run Phillips curve) was due to their omission to take adequate note of the effect of foreign rates of inflation on the formation of expectations of domestic rates of inflation.

Summarising the empirical evidence, it would appear that there is sufficient evidence to sustain monetarists in their belief that $\beta = 1$ so that there would be no trade-off between unemployment and inflation in the long run, but not enough evidence to convince all the sceptics.

4.4.5   *Augmented Phillips curve: concluding remarks*

We would like to stress that the augmented Phillips curve is quite capable of explaining rising unemployment occurring at the same time as accelerating inflation. All that is necessary is to assume that the expected rate of inflation lags behind the actual rate, so that expectations of future inflation rates can still be increasing while excess demand is decreasing (i.e. unemployment will be increasing). Friedman (1977) has also offered an explanation of the existence of a positively sloped Phillips curve for several years which is compatible with the hypothesis that the Phillips curve is vertical in the long run. Points on the vertical Phillips curve require actual inflation to be fully anticipated. With rising rates of inflation, however, Friedman has noted that inflation rates tend to become increasingly volatile and also tend to be accompanied by more government intervention in the price-setting process. Errors occur, therefore, in the formation of expectations, and also relative prices move further away from those that would be set by market forces. Both these factors would permit the simultaneous occurrence of rising unemployment and accelerating inflation as a transitional phenomenon, but, as Friedman has pointed out, the transition period could be quite long, extending over decades.

This completes the survey of the Phillips curve analysis; but, whatever the true value of β it should be apparent that such analysis on its own is unable to explain inflation – just as was the case for the quantity theory approach. In view of the importance of the concept of the natural rate of unemployment, we shall discuss this concept in more detail in the following section.

4.5 The natural rate of unemployment

The natural rate is the pivot around which the actual rate of unemployment moves. It is therefore essential to the analysis that the natural rate is both stable (i.e. slow to change) and independent of the rate of inflation.

4.5.1 *Determinants of the natural rate*

The natural rate of unemployment is associated in monetarist analysis with equilibrium in the labour market and hence in the structure of real wage rates. For example Friedman (1968) has argued:

that the natural rate is dependent upon the structural characteristics of the commodity markets, including market imperfections, stochastic variability in demands and supplies, the cost of gathering information about job vacancies and labour availabilities, the costs of mobility and so on.

Tobin (1972) has argued that, in addition to search unemployment, the natural rate will also depend upon the regional dispersion of unemployment since even when there is upward pressure on wage rates in aggregate there will be unemployment in the less prosperous regions.

4.5.2 *The natural rate and inflation*

The natural rate is generally held to be determined by the structure of the real side of the economy and the institutions of the labour market; but, in contrast, Flemming (1976) has argued that inflation can influence the natural rate in four ways. The first two are linked to wage rigidity. Efficiency of allocation of resources in the labour market requires real wages that are flexible both downwards and upwards, otherwise the market mechanism will not function efficiently. Given money wages that are inflexible downwards, real wages must also be inflexible downwards in the absence of inflation. This is inefficient, so that the natural rate of unemployment will be high. In contrast, inflation permits real wages to fall, and therefore the natural rate will fall as a result of the better allocation of resources in the labour market. On the other hand, inflation may strengthen the trade unions who would be expected to act as an additional frictional factor impeding the operation of the labour market and thus raising the natural rate. The strengthening of trade unions could be due to two factors. First, during the process of inflation some non-unionised labour may fall behind other workers and the resulting discontent encourage them to join unions. Second, since most wage agreements are in money terms, the presence of inflation will cause agreements to be of a short duration. As wage negotiations are time-consuming, it would be expected that such negotiations would be more and more delegated to specialist negotiators.

The other two possible influences suggested are based on the idea of job search. In principle this can be regarded as a type of investment, the return for which is the attainment of a more attractive job, and as such it should be influenced by two factors: the rate of interest and the level of compensation while unemployed. If, as is likely, the nominal rate of interest rises only slowly in response to inflation, then the real rate of interest falls, making for cheaper borrowing. This will lower the cost of being unemployed and consequently will raise the natural rate of unemployment. However, if the unemployed do not borrow to any great extent to finance their unemployment, then this is only likely to play a very minor part in the determination of the natural rate. In contrast the second factor, i.e. compensation for unemployment, could play an important role. If for example unemployment benefits rise automatically in line with inflation and wages do not (i.e. the unemployment benefit-to-wages ratio is raised), the real cost of being unemployed is lowered and the natural rate would be expected to rise. Conversely, if unemployment benefits fall relative to wage levels, the real cost of being unemployed rises and the natural rate should fall.

How strong all these effects are on the natural rate is debatable, and it would seem to be a reasonable approximation to reality to assume that the natural rate is independent of the rate of inflation at least in the short run.

4.5.3   *The natural rate: concluding remarks*

It would also be expected that, if the cost of being unemployed were reduced, the natural rate would increase. One measure of the cost of being unemployed is the benefit-ratio percentage reproduced in the social security statistics. This ratio is defined as (standard rate unemployment benefit plus earnings-related supplement plus family allowances) divided by (average weekly earnings plus family allowances minus income tax minus national insurance contributions). This ratio showed a marked increase over the period 1964–67 (i.e. 1964 = 44.6; 1965 = 49.3; 1966 = 68.6; 1967 = 73.2). It would be reasonable to assume that the natural rate of unemployment also increased over this period and that, therefore, the relationship between excess demand for labour and unemployment changed.

Policy-makers are obviously interested in what level of unemployment is envisaged in the concept of the natural rate. The usual method of estimating the rate is to solve the equation:

$$\dot{W} = f(U) + \dot{P}^e \qquad (4.6)$$

for $f(U)$ subject to the constraint that $\dot{P}^e$ and $\dot{W}$ are equal. Estimates of approximately 2 per cent for the UK were found by Parkin, Sumner and Ward (1975) and between 5 and 6 per cent for the USA by Tobin (1972). Regarding the discrepancy between the estimates for the two countries, it should be remembered that there are differences in (a) methods of measuring unemployment and (b) the structure of the labour markets in the two countries.

4.6   Inflation and the rate of interest

In an analysis similar to that which distinguishes between the market and the natural rate of unemployment, monetarists have revived the classical non-monetary theory of the real rate of interest (the real rate can be defined as the yield on an asset after adjustment for future price changes). In monetarist analysis, real rates of interest are determined by ' . . . a multiplicity of factors traditionally summarised in the phrase productivity and thrift' (Andersen, 1973). Thus, in line with augmented Phillips curve theory discussed earlier in section 4.4, the importance of price expectations is emphasised. In this case the distinction is between nominal or market rates of interest and the real rate of interest, with the real rate being determined by non-monetary factors.

Traditional analysis suggests that an increase in the quantity of money will lower interest rates. In terms of the *IS–LM* model, an increase in the money supply causes the *LM* curve to shift downwards causing a movement downwards along the negative sloped *IS* curve. Similarly in dynamic terms, an increase in the rate of growth of the money supply would produce lower rates of interest.

In contrast, monetarists contend that this is only the initial effect. Increasing the rate of monetary expansion would lead to increasing aggregate demand and income, which would increase the demand for loans and also liquidity preference. In addition, even in the short run some price increases would occur, thus reducing the real value of the money supply. These effects would reverse the initial fall in interest rates. According to monetarist thinking, the increase in the rate of monetary expansion would in the long run lead mainly to an increase in the rate of inflation (see section 4.4). The resulting increases in the actual rates of inflation would lead to upward adjustments by the public of their expectations of future inflation rates. The expected nominal (or market) rates of return on those assets whose yields are fixed in money terms would, therefore, fall relative to those fixed in real terms. Investors would be less willing to hold these assets at lower yields. This would cause the price of these assets to fall and their nominal yields to rise, so as to restore parity (after allowances for risk) between their yields and those fixed in real terms. Hence in equilibrium the following relationship would hold:

$$r_t = i_t + \dot{P}_t^e \tag{4.7}$$

where r = market or nominal rate of interest and i = real rate of interest. In this equilibrium, the real rate of interest is determined by real factors and would be largely independent of monetary changes. During the transitional period, however, changes in the money supply would cause real rates of interest to alter because of the slow adjustment of actual and expected rates of inflation to monetary changes. Again, as noted in section 4.4.5, the transitional period could be quite long.

This relationship has been tested for both the USA and the UK (e.g. Gibson, 1970, and Foster, 1977, who both found some support for the view that inflation expectations have an important role to play in the determination of interest rates).

4.7 Inflation in the open economy

So far the discussion of inflation has implicitly assumed that the economy is closed or self-contained. We shall now relax this assumption and discuss the monetarist explanation of the inflationary process in the context of an open economy. This analysis, however, does depend critically on the type of exchange rate regime in existence, and we shall concentrate first of all on the case of fixed exchange rates.

4.7.1 *Fixed exchange rates*

In a world of fixed exchange rates, monetarists argue that inflation is an international monetary phenomenon which can be explained by an excess demand expectations model, where the excess demand depends on world rather than domestic monetary expansion. Rapid monetary expansion by either a large country relative to the rest of the world or a number of small countries at the same time would result in an increase in the world rate of monetary expansion. This would create excess demand and result in inflationary pressure throughout the world economy. We shall illustrate this process by taking, as an example, the case of rapid monetary expansion by a large country, but noting that this analysis is equally applicable to the case of rapid monetary expansion occurring simultaneously in a number of smaller countries.

Rapid monetary expansion by the large country will lead to that country experiencing a faster rate of inflation than that ruling in the rest of the world. This will result in a balance of payments deficit as its goods became less competitive (see chapter 7 for a detailed discussion of this process, termed 'The Monetary Approach to the Balance of Payments'). Other countries will experience balance of payments surpluses, thus causing an increase in their domestic rates of monetary expansion. In this way the inflationary pressure initiated in the large country will spread to the rest of the world leading to a general, i.e. world-wide, upward revision of expectations of future inflation rates.

As a result of (a) the slowing down in the rate of monetary expansion in the large country owing to the balance of payments deficit and (b) the increase in this rate in other countries because of balance of payments surpluses, balance of payments disequilibria would be eliminated. In the long run, therefore, the inflation rates of the individual countries linked together by a system of fixed exchange rates would tend to converge to a common world average inflation rate.

4.7.2   *Fixed exchange rates: an alternative rationale*

An alternative exposition of the monetarist view of the transmission of inflation between economies is the price transfer mechanism. In contrast with the view enshrined in the monetary approach to the balance of payments, flows of international reserves are regarded in this approach as accommodating, rather than directly initiating, the transfer of inflation. Firms are viewed as setting their own prices after taking into consideration their expectations of prices that other firms are likely to charge for similar goods. If the firm is selling goods in a world-wide market, there is no reason to assume that the firm will confine its expectations to the prices charged by other domestic firms. The expectations relevant to the pricing policy of the firm will, therefore, include the expected pricing policies of both domestic and foreign firms producing similar types of goods.

In the case of inflation owing to domestic excess demand, this approach yields similar predictions to the normal monetary approach to the balance of payments, i.e. a decrease or reduction in the rate of growth of the domestic money supply owing to the balance of payments deficit. It is in the case of the transmission of inflation from abroad that differences arise. As prices rise abroad, domestic firms will revise their prices upwards, and as a result domestic prices can rise without the existence of domestic excess demand. During the adjustment period, the country that is importing inflation will experience monetary expansion owing to the balance of payments surplus, but this accommodates rather than causes the inflation. Here again the analysis predicts convergence of actual inflation rates.

4.7.3   *Inflation rates since 1960*

Up to 1972–73, the major Western economies maintained a system of fixed exchange rates, and it is therefore important to ask how far this monetarist analysis is supported by the inflationary experiences of the countries involved. In figure 4.9 we have plotted the rates of inflation experienced by five industrial countries during the period 1960–77. The salient feature revealed is that, while the levels of inflation experienced by the individual countries may have differed, the general pattern has been remarkably similar. Any explanation of inflation must then be capable of explaining this similarity.

From the end of the Korean War, the broad trend was one of falling inflation rates throughout the Western world until the early 1960s. Monetarists have explained the trend by the adoption of conservative policy measures in the United States during the 1950s which imparted a deflationary influence on the world economy. In the early 1960s however, the United States began to adopt expansionary policy measures which, it is argued, led to the start of the inflationary pressures experienced in the Western world. Reference to figure 4.9 will show that the real impetus to inflationary pressure came in the mid-1960s, which, monetarists claim, was due to an

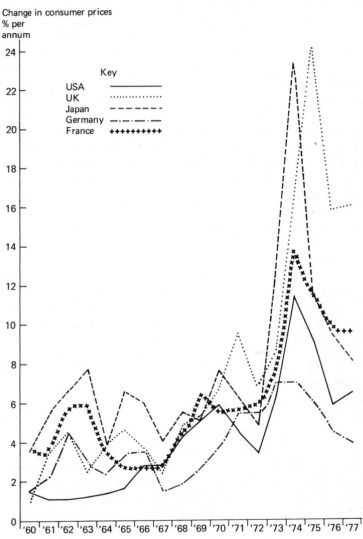

Change in consumer prices
% per annum

Key
USA ——————
UK ·················
Japan — — — —
Germany —··—··—··—
France ++++++++++

Source: *National Institute Economic Review*: Table Consumer Prices.

Figure 4.9

expansion of the money supply in the United States following the financing of the Vietnam War by budget deficits. In line with the mechanism outlined earlier in this section, it is claimed that this inflationary pressure was transmitted to other Western countries via changes in their domestic money supplies originating from the US balance of payments deficit.

Although monetarist analysis can explain the general pattern of inflation rates, figure 4.9 shows that, in contrast to the predictions of the monetary approach, the individual inflation rates experienced during the period of fixed exchange rates (i.e. up to 1972–73) showed no tendency to converge. While it is possible that existing tariffs or non-tariff barriers could help to explain the continued existence of such differences, a more acceptable explanation lies in the distinction between tradable and non-tradable goods.

4.7.4   *The Nordic theory of inflation*

This distinction between traded and non-traded goods forms the basis of the Nordic theory of inflation. Briefly the economy is divided into two sectors, one of which faces foreign competition and the other of which is sheltered because the goods are not traded (see e.g. Edgren, Faxen and Odhner, 1969). The inflation rate of the economy will be a weighted average of the rates of inflation experienced in the tradable-goods sector (T) and in the non-tradable-goods sector (NT).

$$\dot{P} = \lambda \dot{P}_T + (1 - \lambda)\dot{P}_{NT}. \tag{4.8}$$

Abstracting from exchange rate changes, it is argued that the rate of inflation in the tradable-goods sector will be the same as that experienced in the rest of the world (WT).

$$\dot{P}_T = \dot{P}_{WT}. \tag{4.9}$$

This follows from the law of one price, which states that, in the absence of trade barriers and after allowing for transport costs, perfect commodity arbitrage will ensure that the prices for similar traded goods must be the same. The rate of growth of money wages in the tradable-goods sector ($\dot{W}_T$) is assumed to be determined by the rate of inflation in that sector ($\dot{P}_T$), plus the growth of productivity in that sector ($\dot{\Pi}$).

$$\dot{W}_T = \dot{P}_T + \dot{\Pi}_T. \tag{4.10}$$

On the other hand, because of worker solidarity, the rate of growth of money wages in the non-tradable goods sector ($\dot{W}_{NT}$) is assumed to be equal to the rate of growth of money wages in the tradable-goods sector ($\dot{W}_T$), i.e. (4.11). The rate of inflation of non-traded goods will therefore be equal to the rate of wage increase less the growth of productivity ($\dot{\Pi}_{NT}$) in that sector (4.12).

$$\dot{W}_{NT} = \dot{W}_T \tag{4.11}$$

$$\dot{P}_{NT} = \dot{W}_{NT} - \dot{\Pi}_{NT}. \tag{4.12}$$

Substituting (4.12) into (4.8) gives

$$\dot{P} = \lambda \dot{P}_T + (1 - \lambda)(\dot{W}_{NT} - \dot{\Pi}_{NT}). \tag{4.13}$$

From (4.10) and (4.11):

$$\dot{W}_{NT} = \dot{W}_T = \dot{P}_T + \dot{\Pi}_T. \tag{4.14}$$

Therefore, substituting (4.14) into (4.13), we obtain

$$\dot{P} = \lambda \dot{P}_T + (1 - \lambda)(\dot{P}_T + \dot{\Pi}_T - \dot{\Pi}_{NT}). \tag{4.15}$$

Factorising and rearranging finally gives

$$\dot{P} = \dot{P}_T + (1 - \lambda)(\dot{\Pi}_T - \dot{\Pi}_{NT}). \tag{4.16}$$

Thus the average rate of inflation in the country is given by the rate of inflation in tradable goods plus a term representing the differences between the growth of productivity in tradables and non-tradables. It is only if these two growth rates are equal for all countries that the rate of inflation will conform to the average world inflation rate. The Nordic theory of inflation leaves open the causation of inflation of tradable goods. This could be specified to be a function of world monetary expansion (i.e. a monetarist explanation), and in this case the Nordic view becomes a theory of how inflation is transmitted from one country to another. However, while the rate of inflation of tradable goods should be equalised between one country and another, this does not imply that the average rate of inflation of tradables and non-tradables will be equalised. This is due to potential differences between the rates of growth of productivity within the two sectors.

Having discussed the monetarist analysis of inflation within a world of fixed exchange rates, we will now turn to the analysis of pure floating exchange rates which is analogous, in some respects, to that of a closed economy.

4.7.5   *Floating exchange rates*

The rate of domestic inflation will be determined by domestic monetary policy, and any difference between the domestic inflation rate and those being experienced in the rest of the world will cause the exchange rate to adjust. However, differences do arise with respect to the time lag envisaged between monetary expansion and the resulting increase in the rate of inflation. If the individuals operating within financial markets are subject to rational expectations and believe that an increase in monetary expansion will lead to an increase in inflation and therefore to a depreciation in the exchange rate, then the markets will mark down the exchange rate immediately without waiting for the gradual adjustment process to take place. Assuming that the foreign currency price of imports is given, the domestic currency price of imports will rise as the exchange rate depreciates. Thus the time lag between monetary expansion and the resulting rise in the rate of inflation is curtailed.

It is claimed that a pure floating exchange rate regime will provide an economy with complete insulation from foreign experience of inflation, but Laidler (1977) has claimed that this depends critically on how expectations with respect to future rates are formed. This can be demonstrated by referring to equations (4.17) and (4.18) below, which are typically monetarist in their formulation. Equation (4.17) is simply the augmented Phillips curve and (4.18) describes the determination of the exchange rate using the law of one price; and, for ease of exposition, no distinction is made between traded and non-traded goods.

$$\dot{P} = f(U) + \dot{P}^e \tag{4.17}$$

$$E = P/P_W \tag{4.18}$$

where E = the exchange rate, i.e. the domestic currency price of foreign currency; P = the domestic price level in terms of domestic currency; and P_W = the world price level in terms of foreign currency. If $\dot{P}^e$ is determined purely by domestic variables, then an economy is completely insulated from foreign price changes both in the short and the long run. These will operate only on the exchange rate via equation (4.18), and the domestic general price level will be determined by domestic monetary expansion. If, however, expectations of inflation are formed with reference not only to domestic influences but also to expected movements in foreign price levels and in the exchange rate, then it is only in the special case where expectations regarding potential exchange rate changes and foreign prices are formed in the same way (rational expectations) or at the same speed (adaptive expectations) that complete insulation will occur in the short run. In this special case, expected changes in the world price level will produce corresponding changes in the exchange rate leaving the domestic price level unchanged via equation (4.18). Otherwise expectations of foreign price changes will influence $\dot{P}^e$, which will in turn influence the domestic rate of inflation through equation (4.17).

Referring back again to figure 4.9, it is notable that, although there is some tendency for the development of a greater variation between the inflation rates of the individual countries, the similarity of the pattern of their rates continues after the breakdown of the fixed exchange rate regime. This can be explained by the fact that the exchange rate regime in existence since 1972 has not been a pure float, but rather a managed float with significant degrees of intervention by the various national authorities. Thus, instead of the exchange rate adjusting completely so that the official financing section of the balance of payments was equal to zero, changes in domestic inflation rates following monetary changes have been partly reflected in exchange rate changes and partly in balance of payments deficits/surpluses. Therefore, the international transmission of inflation through monetary changes via the balance of payments has still operated to produce some conformity among the individual inflation rates, though, of course, to a lesser degree than during the fixed exchange rate system.

4.8 Conclusions

In this chapter we have discussed the monetarist contention that inflation is always and everywhere a monetary phenomenon and have seen that this view of inflation offers an explanation as to why the patterns of inflation in the individual countries have tended to follow similar trends. The distinction between tradable and non-tradable goods predicts that, while the trends have been similar, there is no reason to expect convergence of the various inflation rates. It is however only fair to point out that monetarists are not the only ones to recognise the similarity of inflation rates. A socio-logical explanation would probably have recourse to demonstration effects, i.e. militant trade unions in one country being copied by trade unions in other countries. The problem with this explanation is to explain why militancy rather than docility was copied, and also to explain the speed-up of inflation rates in 1967. Monetarists contend that it is difficult to conceive of sociological factors that declined throughout the 1950s to produce declining rates of inflation, then strengthened again in the early 1960s to produce the rising trends in inflation rates observed in figure 4.9. As noted earlier, inflation rates speeded up from 1967 onwards and again from 1972, with a temporary dip in 1971. Monetarists argue that it is difficult to identify sociological factors which could vary in this manner. In contrast the monetarist explanation via the excess demand/expecta-tions model is capable of explaining such trends, and broad cycles around the trends, in terms of variations in the rate of monetary expansion.

If the monetarist explanation of inflation is correct, it is necessary to explain why governments have permitted excessive monetary expansion. On the assumption that governments are not ignorant of the consequences of excessive monetary expansion, they must tolerate inflation because they believe that there are benefits to be derived from monetary expansion. Among the benefits likely to accrue are political gains from a lower rate of interest (at least in the short run), thus lowering both the cost of financing government debt and also the cost of mortgages for house purchase. Similarly, unemployment levels may be lowered and at the same time inflation may increase government tax revenue (i.e. the inflation tax). An additional advantage is that inflation reduces the real value of any outstanding government debt whose value is fixed in nominal terms. However, if the monetarist viewpoint examined in this chapter is correct, some of these benefits will be short-term only, but this short term may be sufficient for electoral purposes.

Appendix 1: Expectations

In many economic relationships the variable relevant to economic units is the value that that variable is expected to take, rather than its actual value, at any point of time. Therefore, it is of great importance to examine how expectations are formed. Within the literature, two hypotheses concerning the formation of expectations have been widely used. These are (a) adaptive expectations and (b) rational expectations. Following Hicks (1946), we note that three types of information are relevant to the formation of price expectations: (a) non-economic events, such as the weather, war, etc.; (b) the actual history of previous price changes; and (c) structural economic changes such as changes in monetary and fiscal policy. Adaptive expectations refers to information of the second type and rational expectations to the third type of information.

A4.1 Adaptive expectations

A4.1.1 Nature of adaptive expectations

The basic idea behind the adaptive expectations hypothesis is that expectations are revised each period by a constant fraction $(0 < \Phi < 1)$ of the discrepancy between the latest observed value of the variable (Y_{t-1}) and the value of Y expected for that period (Y_{t-1}^*), but made at the previous time period $(t - 2)$. In other words expectations are revised by a constant fraction of the latest error made $(Y_{t-1} - Y_{t-1}^*)$. More formally:

$$Y_t^* - Y_{t-1}^* = \Phi(Y_{t-1} - Y_{t-1}^*). \tag{A4.1}$$

Equation (A4.1) can be factorised and rearranged to derive equation (A4.2):

$$Y_t^* = \Phi Y_{t-1} + (1 - \Phi)Y_{t-1}^*. \tag{A4.2}$$

This formulation emphasises the fact that the value Y is expected to take in period t is a weighted average of the actual value for the previous period and the value expected to occur in that period. If $\Phi = 1$, the expected value always equals the actual value occurring in period $t - 1$. On the other hand, if $\Phi = 0$, then the expected value for period t equals the value expected to exist in period $t - 1$, i.e. the expected value of the variable Y is constant for all periods.

If equation (A4.2) is lagged one period we obtain:

$$Y_{t-1}^* = \Phi Y_{t-2} + (1 - \Phi)Y_{t-2}^*. \tag{A4.3}$$

Multiplying equation (A4.3) by $(1 - \Phi)$ gives

$$(1 - \Phi)Y^*_{t-1} = \Phi(1 - \Phi)Y_{t-2} + (1 - \Phi)^2 Y^*_{t-2} \tag{A4.4}$$

If equation (A4.4) is substituted into equation (A4.2) we obtain:

$$Y^*_t = \Phi Y_{t-1} + \Phi(1 - \Phi)Y_{t-2} + (1 - \Phi)^2 Y^*_{t-2} \tag{A4.5}$$

In a similar manner, repeated back substitution can be used to obtain:

$$Y^*_t = \Phi Y_{t-1} + \Phi(1 - \Phi)Y_{t-2} + \cdots + \Phi(1 - \Phi)^{n-1} Y_{t-n}. \tag{A4.6}$$

From equation (A4.6) it can be seen that the expected value of the variable is a geometrically weighted average of past observed values of that variable. The weights are Φ, $\Phi(1 - \Phi), \ldots, \Phi(1 - \Phi)^{n-1}$ respectively, and these form a geometric series with the ratio $(1 - \Phi)$. If this series is summed to infinity, the sum is 1, i.e. the weights sum to unity.

A4.1.2   Problems with adaptive expectations

Adaptive expectations is a very mechanical method of forming expectations about any variable. Economic units are assumed to follow a rule-of-thumb approach so that they never take into consideration other additional information that may become available. This particular defect shows up where the variable about which expectations are being formed has a trend over time. From equation (A4.1) it can be seen that if Y is rising steadily over time (i.e. $Y_t > Y_{t-1}$), then Y^* can only do so (i.e. $Y^*_t > Y^*_{t-1}$) if Y^*_{t-1} is less than Y_{t-1}. Since from equation (A4.2) Y^*_t is the weighted average of Y_{t-1} and Y^*_{t-1}, Y^*_t must also be less than Y_{t-1}. This means that, despite the observed trend increases in Y, the value of Y expected in period $t - 1$ to occur in period t (i.e. Y^*_t) is less than the observed value in that period.

A4.2   Rational expectations

A4.2.1   Nature of rational expectations

The basis of rational expectations is that expectations are formed as if the correct economic model had been used to predict future values of the variable concerned. Purely for sake of exposition, we shall assume that the current rate of inflation is a function solely of the lagged rate of monetary expansion. According to the rational expectations hypothesis, expectations of future rates of inflation will then be determined by the current and previous rates of monetary expansion.

A4.2.2   Problems of rational expectations

Two problems arise with this hypothesis of how expectations are formed: (1) the determination of the correct model and (2) the cost of obtaining information.

The first problem can be illustrated with respect to the formation of expectations about inflation. Should a monetarist believe expectations of future rates of inflation are formed on the basis of recent rates of monetary expansion, even though he knows some people believe that inflation is attributable to sociological factors? In a weaker version of the rational expectations hypothesis, allowance is made in the short run for the influence of incorrect economic models. In the long run, however, those agents would recognise the deficiencies of their model of the economy and would form their expectations according to the predictions of the correct model.

The second problem is that information is often costly to obtain. (This forms the basis of the distinction made by Feige and Pearce (1976) between economically rational expectations and rational expectations.) In such instances, it could be rational for expectations to be formed according to some rule-of-thumb method such as adaptive expectations. It is inconsistent with rational expectations if this rule is followed when current experience has shown it to be incorrect. This would occur, for example, if the variable concerned was subject to trend increases or decreases.

A4.2.3 A synthesis

Flemming (1976) has suggested a synthesis of the rational expectations and adaptive expectations hypotheses. If no time trend exists, economic units would form expectations adaptively about future price levels. However, once the price level showed a consistent trend of increase, agents would form expectations about the rate of inflation. Expectations about the future price level would be obtained by applying the expected rate of inflation to the current price level. Similarly, if the rate of inflation increased, expectations would then be formed about the rate of acceleration of inflation. Expectations about the rate of inflation and the price level respectively would be obtained by applying the expected rate of acceleration of inflation to the current rate of inflation, and then the derived expected rate of inflation to the current price level. This combination of the two hypotheses would be consistent with economic agents using rule-of-thumb methods to avoid costs of searching for relevant information but taking into consideration such additional information as is readily available. The problems of the adaptive expectations hypothesis discussed in section A4.1.2 above would be avoided.

Bibliography

*Titles marked * are particularly recommended for student reading.*

Andersen, L. C. (1973), 'The State of the Monetarist Debate'. *Federal Reserve Bank of St Louis Review*, vol. 56 (September).

Cagan, P. (1956), 'The Monetary Dynamics of Hyperinflation'. In *Studies in the Quantity Theory of Money*, edited by M. Friedman (Chicago: University Press).

Carlson, J. A. and Parkin, J. M. (1975), 'Inflation Expectations'. *Economica*, vol. 42 (May).

Cross, R. B. and Laidler, D. E. W. (1975), 'Inflation, Excess Demand and Expectations in Fixed Exchange Rate Open Economies: Some Preliminary Empirical Results'. In *Inflation in the World Economy*, edited by J. M. Parkin and G. Zis (Manchester: University Press).

Edgren, G., Faxen, K. O. and Odhner, G. E. (1969), 'Wage Growth and the Distribution of Income'. *Swedish Journal of Economics*, vol. 71.

Feige, E. L. and Pearce, D. K. (1976), 'Economically Rational Expectations: Are Innovations in the Rate of Inflation Independent of Innovations in Measures of Monetary and Fiscal Policy?' *Journal of Political Economy*, vol. 84 (June).

Flemming, J. (1976), *Inflation* (Oxford: University Press).

Foster, J. (1977), 'Tests of the Simple Fisher Hypothesis Utilising Observed Inflationary Expectations: Some Further Evidence'. *Scottish Journal of Political Economy*, vol. 24 (November).

Friedman, M. (1956), 'The Quantity Theory of Money – A Restatement'. In *Studies in the Quantity Theory of Money*, edited by M. Friedman (Chicago: University Press).

Friedman, M. (1968), 'The Role of Monetary Policy'. *American Economic Review*, vol. 58 (March).

Friedman, M. (1970), *The Counter-Revolution in Monetary Theory*. IEA Occasional Paper, no. 33 (London: Institute of Economic Affairs).

*Friedman, M. (1975), *Unemployment versus Inflation? An Evaluation of the Phillips Curve*. IEA Occasional Paper, no. 44 (London: Institute of Economic Affairs).

Friedman, M. (1977), 'Inflation and Unemployment'. *Journal of Political Economy*, vol. 85 (June).

Gibson, W. (1970), 'Price Expectations Effects on Interest Rates'. *Journal of Finance*, vol. 25 (March).

Harrod, R. F. (1972), 'The Issues: Five Views'. In *Inflation as a Global Problem*, edited by R. Hinshaw (London: John Hopkins Press).

Hicks, J. R. (1946), *Value and Capital* (Oxford: University Press).

Hicks, J. R. (1975), 'The Permissive Economy'. In *Crisis '75 . . . ?* IEA Occasional Paper Special, no. 43 (London: Institute of Economic Affairs).

Laidler, D. E. W. (1977), 'Expectations and the Behaviour of Prices under Flexible Exchange Rates'. *Economica*, vol. 44 (November).

*Laidler, D. E. W. and Parkin, J. M. (1975), 'Inflation: A Survey'. *Economic Journal*, vol. 85 (December).

Lipsey, R. G. (1960), 'The Relationship Between Unemployment and the Rate of Change of Money Wage Rates in the U.K. 1862–1957: A Further Analysis'. *Economica*, vol. 27 (February).

Parkin, J. M. (1977), 'Inflation without Growth: A Long-Run Perspective on Short-Run Stabilisation Policies'. In *Stabilisation of the Domestic and International Economy*, edited by K. Brunner and A. H. Meltzer; issued as a supplement to *Journal of Monetary Economics 1977*.

Parkin, J. M., Sumner, M. T. and Ward, R. (1975), 'The Effects of Excess Demand, Generalised Expectations and Wage-Price Controls on Wage Inflation in the UK'. In *Proceedings of the Conference on Wage and Price Controls at Rochester University*, edited by K. Brunner and A. H. Meltzer. (New York: North Holland.)

Phelps, E. S. (1968), 'Money Wage Dynamics and Labour Market Equilibrium'. *Journal of Political Economy*, vol. 76 (August).

Phelps-Brown, H. (1975), 'A Non-Monetarist View of the Pay Explosion'. *Three Banks Review* (March).

Phillips, A. W. (1958), 'The Relation between Unemployment and the Rate of Change of Money Wage Rates in the United Kingdom, 1861–1957'. *Economica*, vol. 25 (November).

Saunders, P. G. and Nobay, A. R. (1972), 'Price Expectations, the Phillips Curve and Incomes Policy'. In *Incomes Policy and Inflation*, edited by J. M. Parkin and M. T. Sumner (Manchester: University Press).

Solow, R. M. (1969), *Price Expectations and the Behaviour of the Price Level* (Manchester: University Press).

Tobin, J. (1972), 'Inflation and Unemployment'. *American Economic Review*, vol. 62 (March).

*Trevithick, J. A. and Mulvey, C. (1975), *The Economics of Inflation* (London: Martin Robertson).

Turnovsky, S. J. (1972), 'The Expectations Hypothesis and the Aggregate Wage Equation: Some Empirical Evidence for Canada'. *Economica*, vol. 39 (February).

Wiles, P. (1973), 'Cost Inflation and the State of Economic Theory'. *Economic Journal*, vol. 83 (June).

5 Monetary Policy

In this chapter we will discuss monetarist views concerning the conduct and role of monetary policy. These can be considered at two distinct levels. First, there is the question of the optimum conduct of monetary policy and three aspects of this subject will be examined:

(1) the choice of an appropriate target, in section 5.1;
(2) the choice of an indicator, in section 5.2; and
(3) the controversy surrounding the proposal to adopt a monetary rule, in section 5.3.

Second, there is the problem of how to adjust to the optimum monetary policy if monetary expansion has been excessive in the preceding period. This is purely a transitional problem in moving from a situation where the rate of monetary growth is uncontrolled to one where it is controlled. This latter aspect of monetary policy is discussed in section 5.4.

5.1   The appropriate target of monetary policy

Both for a closed economy and also an open economy with floating exchange rates, monetarists contend that the appropriate target of monetary policy should be control of the money supply, rather than control of either the level or structure of interest rates or credit availability. In the case of an open economy with fixed exchange rates, as was pointed out in chapter 3, control of the money supply by the authorities is not possible. In this case the appropriate target of monetary policy should be control of domestic credit expansion.

Direct credit controls are often advocated on the grounds that anyone who borrows money does so to finance expenditure. Controlling credit should therefore control aggregate demand. However, controlling credit is not the same as controlling the money supply. If banks possess reserves over and above those required by the reserve–asset ratio imposed on them, they will attempt to expand their deposits. Even though the authorities impose controls over the volume of their lending to the private sector, the banks can still increase the level of their deposits (i.e. the money supply) by buying securities. This would cause rates of interest to fall. Any increase in the money supply over and above that demanded at existing levels of income and interest rates would cause disequilibrium in the money market. Equilibrium would be restored as these excess money balances are disposed of through the purchase of securities, extra deposits with financial intermediaries, or increased lending via uncontrolled channels. All these effects would cause interest rates to fall and aggregate demand to increase. This analysis suggests that control of credit availability is not the appropriate target of monetary policy. Monetarists also dislike credit controls because they interfere with the operation of the market mechanism. It is felt that any such interference would lead to a misallocation of resources and consequently to inefficiency. Having discussed the role of credit availability as a potential target of monetary policy, we will now examine the question of whether interest rates or the quantity of money should be controlled.

At the broad macroeconomic level the *IS–LM* model for a closed economy can be used to clarify the nature of the choice of the appropriate target of monetary policy. The choice between controlling either the money supply or the level of interest rates will depend upon the relative importance of random disturbances occurring from the real and monetary sectors of the economy. Poole (1970) has shown that if the real side of the economy is more unstable then a money stock target is preferable, whereas if the monetary side of the economy is more unstable then an interest rate target is to be preferred. The analysis underlying these conclusions is discussed and illustrated in figures 5.1 and 5.2, where it is assumed that the objective of policy is to minimise the variance of income about the desired level of Y^*.

5.1.1 *Stochastic monetary disturbances*

In the analysis that follows, the money supply is assumed to be constant so that the random shifts that occur in the *LM* curve are due entirely to unpredictable changes in the demand for money; i.e., the demand for money function is assumed to be unstable. The position of the *IS* curve is taken to be fixed because the underlying behavioural relationships (i.e. the consumption and investment functions) are assumed to be extremely stable. This is illustrated in figure 5.1. For example, if the demand for money increased unexpectedly, the *LM* curve would shift upwards to the left (to LM_1),

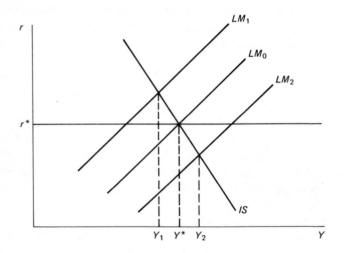

Figure 5.1

so that with the money stock held constant the interest rate would rise and as a result income fall from Y^* to Y_1. Conversely, if the demand for money decreased, the *LM* curve would shift downwards to the right to LM_2, so that income would rise to Y_2, provided the money stock was held constant. Given stochastic monetary disturbances, income will fluctuate between Y_1 and Y_2, if the money stock is held constant.

In contrast, if the authorities pursued a policy of stabilising the rate of interest at r^*, income would be stabilised at the desired level of Y^*. For example, if the demand for money increased unexpectedly, the authorities could increase the supply of money, thus causing the money supply to become endogenous. The increased demand for money would be met and both the rate of interest and income would be stabilised at r^* and Y^* respectively. The opposite policy would be appropriate in the case of a decrease in the demand for money. The authorities would decrease the money supply and income would again be stabilised at Y^* and the rate of interest at r^*. Although we have assumed in figure 5.1 that the position of the *IS* curve is fixed, the same general result (i,e. that an interest rate target is preferable to a money supply target) holds when both curves are subject to random disturbances, provided the expenditure function is less unstable than the demand for money function.

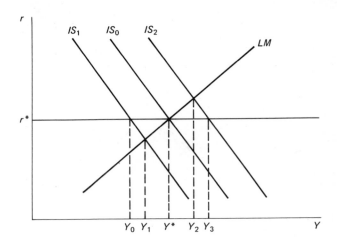

Figure 5.2

5.1.2 *Stochastic real disturbances*

We have described in figure 5.2 the opposite case, where the demand for money function is stable (predictable) while the *IS* curve is subject to unknown random disturbances. These random disturbances are illustrated by stochastic shifts in the IS_0 curve from IS_1

to IS_2. Here again it should be noted that the same analysis applies in the case where both curves shift, provided the demand for money function is less unstable than the expenditure function.

If the quantity of money is held constant the automatic stabilising effect of interest rate movements will limit income fluctuations to between Y_1 and Y_2. In contrast, if the rate of interest is stabilised at r^*, income will fluctuate to a greater extent, i.e. between Y_0 and Y_3. The latter outcome occurs because, in the face of income fluctuations, attempts by the authorities to stabilise the rate of interest at r^* would lead to perverse money supply responses. This is illustrated in figure 5.3. In order to stabilise the rate of interest in the face of an expansionary real disturbance (IS_0 to IS_2) the authorities would have to increase the money supply (LM_0 to LM_2). Conversely, in the case of a contractionary real disturbance (IS_0 to IS_1) the authorities would have to decrease the money supply (LM_0 to LM_1).

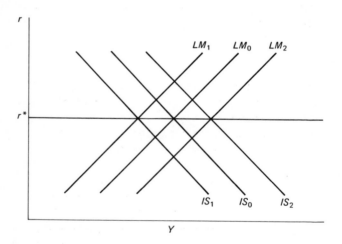

Figure 5.3

It should be noted finally that the extent to which income will vary about the desired level of Y^* will depend not only on the target pursued by the authorities, but also on the relative slopes of the IS and LM curves. For example, where the IS curve is subject to unknown random disturbances and a stable demand for money function exists (figure 5.2), it becomes less critical that the supply of money is controlled the steeper the *LM* curve is relative to the *IS* curve. This is because the variance of income about the desired level will be reduced.

5.1.3 *Control of real or nominal rates of interest*

There is an additional difficulty that arises with regard to the pursuit of an interest rate target. The rate of interest that is relevant for expenditure decisions and therefore the position of the *IS* curve is a real rate of interest. Monetarists argue that the authorities at best are only able to fix the nominal rate of interest. In their non-monetary theory of the real rate of interest they emphasise the importance of price expectations in distinguishing between nominal market rates of interest and real rates of interest. The nominal and real rate will be brought into equality only if the expected rate of inflation is zero. This is a further argument advanced by monetarists to support their preference for a money stock target.

5.1.4 *Concluding remarks*

For the reasons discussed in sections 5.1.1–5.1.3 above, monetarists advocate that the appropriate target for monetary policy should be the control of the money supply. Control of the money supply, as opposed to control of interest rates, would in consequence exercise a considerable stabilising influence on the economy.

5.2 The choice of an indicator

Closely linked to the preference for a money stock target is the problem of the control of the money supply (examined in chapter 3) and the choice of an indicator that will indicate quickly and accurately the thrust (direction and magnitude) of monetary policy. To meet these requirements an indicator must possess certain characteristics. First, it should possess a high degree of correlation with the target variable. Second, accurate and reliable statistics on the indicator should be available quickly to the authorities. Third, the authorities should be capable of controlling the variable; i.e. it should be exogenous rather than endogenous.

One potential indicator is the money supply itself. Statistics on the money supply are usually available at discrete intervals. However, at any particular time the money supply may be responding to prior changes in the monetary base and it would therefore be a poor indicator of current monetary policy. In chapter 3 we discussed the monetarist assertion that the authorities can control the money supply by controlling the monetary base, and we also examined in section 3.4.4 the policy implications of such a choice. Related to their analysis of the money supply process, monetarists prescribe the monetary or reserve base as the most appropriate indicator of monetary policy. The monetary base is advocated as it is potentially under the control of the authorities. In addition, as we examined in chapter 3, it is asserted that any change in the total stock of reserve assets will have a powerful and predictable effect on the money stock, thereby indicating the thrust of monetary policy.

Monetarists do not consider interest rates to be a good indicator of the state of monetary policy. High and low interest rates are traditionally associated with tight and expansionary monetary policies respectively. In contrast, monetarists argue that, while an increase in the rate of monetary growth at first tends to lower nominal interest rates, the initial downward pressure on nominal interest rates will be reversed. This process takes place as spending increases so that inflation accelerates and inflationary expectations are revised upwards. In line with the analysis discussed in chapter 4, this will raise the nominal rate of interest. Therefore the result of an expansionary monetary policy would be to lower rates of interest in the short run but raise them in the long run. The result of a contractionary monetary policy would be precisely opposite to those described above. In consequence, rising or falling nominal interest rates are considered to be a misleading indicator of the direction and magnitude of monetary policy.

The choice of an indicator (total stock of reserves forming the reserve base) and a target (money stock) are therefore closely related. So too is the monetarist view that the authorities should follow some monetary rule and not attempt to use monetary policy in a discretionary manner to control the economy.

5.3 Specifying the nature of the money supply target

It is worthwhile explaining at this stage that a discretionary monetary policy is one where the strength of the policy is varied in a counter-cyclical way according to prevailing economic circumstances. For example, if unemployment rose the rate of monetary expansion would be increased, while if inflation accelerated the rate of monetary expansion would be decreased. Discretionary monetary policy could be either a rough or a fine tuning policy. Rough tuning occurs where policy is varied, but only occasionally and in response to large changes in employment or the rate of inflation. Fine tuning implies the attempt to control closely the economy, responding to small divergences of employment or the rate of inflation from their target values. An alternative policy is to decide on a rule that is believed to be optimal in the long run and then adhere to that rule irrespective of prevailing circumstances.

The question of whether the authorities should follow a monetary rule or adopt a discretionary monetary policy will be decisively influenced by the time lag between monetary policy actions and their effects on economic activity. If this time lag is of a constant length, then in principle the problem could be overcome by forecasting the future time path of income and other variables. The necessary corrective action would be taken after due allowance for the time lag involved with monetary changes. Monetarists argue that, not only is this time lag long, but that it is also variable and this makes the problem for the policy-maker much more difficult. In this section we will review the empirical evidence concerning the time lag between monetary policy actions and their effects on economic activity.

5.3.1 *Time lag*

One of the earliest studies with regard to this time lag was carried out by Friedman (1958 and subsequently 1961). Friedman analysed time series data and compared rates of monetary growth with turning points in the level of economic activity for the United States. On the average of eighteen non-war cycles since 1870, he found that

(a) peaks (turning-points) in the rate of change of the money supply had preceded peaks in the level of economic activity by an average of sixteen months and (b) troughs in the rate of change of the money supply had preceded troughs in the level of economic activity by an average of twelve months. He also found that there was a great deal of variation between business cycles, with a standard deviation of six to seven months for the time lag between turning-points in the rate of change of the money supply and the level of economic activity.

These particular studies have been questioned and criticised by Culbertson (1960, 1961) and by Kareken and Solow (1963) on both methodological and statistical grounds. With regard to the first point they have questioned whether the association found between money and economic activity justifies the inference of a causal relationship. Statistical criticisms were also levied at the way Friedman measured the time lag by analysing turning-points in the rate of change of the money supply against the level of economic activity. Re-running the tests with Friedman's data, but using rates of change for both money and economic activity, Kareken and Solow found no uniform lead of monetary changes over changes in the level of economic activity. They concluded therefore that the two move approximately simultaneously.

Although most of the empirical studies have been carried out for the United States, there have also been a number of studies involving other countries. For example, in a study of the UK Crockett (1970) concluded that movements in the money supply generally preceded movements in money income, but that the pattern of this lead–lag relationship was bi-modal. Crockett found that there was a fairly strong correlation between the money supply and money income, when the money supply had a very short lead over money income (two to three months). There was a further peak in correlation, with a longer time lag, with changes in the money supply leading changes in money income by between twelve and fifteen months. Despite the disagreement about the findings that have come from the various studies involving different data, time periods and countries, practically all the empirical studies have found that changes in the money supply lead changes in nominal income, while the length of the lead (time lag) has varied quite considerably.

Friedman (1970) has summarised the monetarist view by stating that there is a consistent relationship between the rate of growth of the money supply and the rate of growth of nominal income. On average, a change in the rate of monetary growth, if sustained for more than a few months, produces a change in the rate of growth of nominal income about six to nine months later. The initial effects normally show up primarily in real output, with price changes occurring twelve to eighteen months after the increase in the rate of monetary expansion. These relationships are not considered to be precise and the way in which a change in nominal income (timing and extent) is divided between price and output changes depends on the initial conditions at the time of a change in the rate of monetary expansion. The three initial conditions considered to be of major importance are (1) the level of resource utilization; (2) the rate at which unemployment is changing; and (3) the expected rate of inflation. For example, a given rate of monetary expansion would be expected to influence real output more strongly the higher the level of unemployment. Also, the longer inflation has been in existence, the shorter the time lag would be between a further increase in the rate of monetary expansion and an acceleration in the rate of inflation. This would be particularly true in a world of floating exchange rates where, as discussed in chapter 4, an increase in the rate of monetary expansion could lead to an almost immediate depreciation in the exchange rate and therefore to rising prices of imports. This, in turn, would quickly cause a rise in the rate of inflation.

5.3.2 *The rules versus discretion debate*

Monetarists contend that, because of the length and variability of the time lags involved with monetary policy, the rate of growth of the money supply should not be varied in a discretionary manner in response to short-run fluctuations in the level of economic activity. They believe that the consequences of varying the rate of monetary growth cannot be predicted with sufficient accuracy, in the current state of economic knowledge, to permit successful fine tuning, and that discretionary policy could turn out to be destabilising.

A further argument against the use of discretionary monetary policy is the monetarist view, discussed in chapter 4, that the authorities can peg the level of unemployment only in the short run. By engaging in a discretionary monetary expansion the authorities could temporarily reduce the level of unemployment when it rose above the target level adopted by the authorities. Similarly, a discretionary monetary contraction could be used if the level of unemployment fell below the target. Monetarists contend that, if this target level of unemployment is below the natural rate, accelerating inflation will occur. This problem for the authorities is compounded by the fact that they cannot precisely ascertain the value of the natural rate. According to monetarist analysis, it is therefore extremely difficult for the authorities to use a discretionary policy to fine-tune the economy, even if their target is the natural rate of unemployment.

Monetarists also believe that the rate of growth of the money supply should not be varied rapidly and that the monetary authorities should avoid sharp swings in policy. Friedman (1968) has stated that by avoiding sharp swings in monetary policy the authorities can prevent money from being a major source of economic disturbances and has recommended the adoption of a simple monetary rule in the conduct of monetary policy.

The rational expectations literature (discussed more fully in the appendix to chapter 4) provides an additional reason for the adoption of a monetary rule. The belief that the Phillips curve is vertical in the long run implies that an expansionary monetary policy can reduce unemployment below the natural rate, only because the resulting inflation is unexpected. As soon as the inflation is fully expected, it will be incorporated into wage bargains and unemployment will return to the natural rate. The assumption underlying this analysis is that expectations adjust to the actual rate of inflation only gradually. In fact, it is the existence of this time gap between the increase in the actual rate of inflation and the increase in the expected rate that permits a temporary reduction in unemployment below the natural rate. However, if expectations are formed rationally and economic agents have access to the same information as the authorities, the expected rate of inflation will rise immediately in response to an increased rate of monetary expansion. In this case the authorities would be powerless to influence real output by monetary policy, because there would be no lag between the actual and expected rates of inflation. For some monetarists this analysis provides an additional reason for abandoning counter-cyclical policy and concentrating on the generation of a fixed rate of monetary expansion.

S. Fischer (1977) has argued that wage contracts are fixed for a discrete time period and that, therefore, immediate adjustment to an increased expected rate of inflation is impossible. This stickiness of money wages would, it is believed, give monetary policy the power to influence output but only temporarily. Monetary policy would still be powerless to influence long-run conditions. Moreover, radical alterations in monetary policy would lead to attempts to renegotiate wage contracts, and therefore a fixed rate of monetary growth would still seem to be a sensible policy despite stickiness of money wages.

It should be noted that a monetary rule is not submitted as a panacea to fluctuations in the level of economic activity. It is granted that instability in the economy may arise from sources other than the mismanagement of the money supply, but it is believed that the adoption of a monetary rule would remove the greatest source of instability, i.e. random variations in the money supply. Furthermore, by adopting a monetary rule, a built-in stabiliser would be created to deal with short-run cyclical fluctuations in income, although this would necessitate the acceptance of quite large short-run fluctuations in interest rates.

Several rules have been suggested, but perhaps the best known and most widely discussed is the rule proposed by Friedman for the United States. Friedman has argued that the money supply should be expanded at a fixed rate of between 3 and 5 per cent per annum in line with the long-run growth potential of the US economy. It is argued that if the money supply were expanded at such a fixed rate it would satisfy the increased demand for money arising out of, for example, such factors as the growth of output. This would ensure that the price level would be reasonably stable over the decades ahead.

5.4 The period of transition

5.4.1 *The cost of reducing inflation*

If the rate of monetary expansion has been considerably higher than that envisaged in the rule, there will be problems for the authorities in implementing a fixed-rule policy. It was pointed out in chapter 1 that monetarists assert that the basic sources of short-run economic instability are monetary actions, which result in accelerations or decelerations in the rate of monetary growth. If, in the preceding period, the rate of monetary growth were 20 per cent per annum, then reducing the rate to 15 per cent would have a contractionary effect on nominal income. Laidler (1971) has used the analysis underlying the Phillips curve to illustrate the dilemma facing the authorities. The analysis is presented in figure 5.4, which depicts a long-run Phillips curve which is not vertical. This emphasises that the result in no way depends on the existence of a Phillips curve that is vertical in the long run.

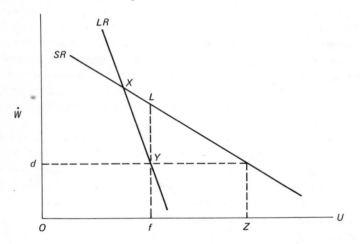

Figure 5.4

In figure 5.4 the curve marked *LR* is the long-run Phillips curve and the curve marked *SR* the short-run Phillips curve dependent on the level of inflation expected to prevail. The initial starting position is *X*, which is both a short- and long-run equilibrium situation. Assume that the rate of inflation entailed at *X* is too high for the authorities' liking and that they wish to move to position *Y* on the long-run curve (where $\dot{W} = Od$, and $U = Of$).

In order to examine the cost of reducing the rate of increase of money wages (and hence the rate of inflation), we shall examine the two extreme policy options open to the authorities to move to their preferred position at Y. The first is to raise unemployment to OZ so that the rate of wage inflation would fall to Od, i.e. a movement along the short-run Phillips curve. In accordance with the analysis discussed in chapter 4, as the actual level of inflation fell below the expected level, the short-run Phillips curve would shift downwards so that unemployment would eventually fall to Of and both a short- and long-run equilibrium would occur at Y. However, the authorities could follow an alternative policy of increasing unemployment to Of so that the initial movement along the short-run Phillips curve would be to L. As before, the actual rate of inflation would fall below the expected rate (but to a lesser extent) so that the short-run Phillips curve would again move downwards, but the adjustment under this policy would be much slower than under the first policy. The authorities could of course follow a compromise between these two policies, but the dilemma always facing them is that the more rapidly inflation is reduced the higher will be the cost in terms of unemployment. Recognition of this fact has led monetarists to advocate a very gradual adjustment process, so that the rate of monetary expansion is slowly brought down to the desired level envisaged by the prescribed monetary rule.

This type of policy entails living with inflation for quite long periods of time and monetarists have suggested that some form of indexation would be a useful policy measure to accompany the gradual adjustment to a lower rate of inflation (e.g. Friedman, 1974).

5.4.2 *Indexation*

Indexation takes the form of adjusting the size of debts fixed in money terms to remove the effects of price changes induced by inflation. In this way the real value of economic variables, such as money wages and the nominal rate of interest, are preserved regardless of the actual rate of price inflation.

The slower the adjustment to a lower rate of inflation, the higher will be the total cost of inflation incurred through arbitrary redistribution of income and wealth. It is claimed that indexation will drastically reduce this cost and make it easier to live with inflation for the long periods of time envisaged in the gradual adjustment process. It is also claimed that indexation would assist the adjustment process by reducing the temporary increase in unemployment necessary to achieve a lower rate of inflation. Employers and employees would bargain in terms of real wages, confident that any change in the rate of inflation would cause money wages to be adjusted automatically. This would remove the danger of employers being committed to excessive money wage increases when in fact the rate of inflation declined. In this case, employers would decrease their labour force and unemployment would increase. In contrast, with indexation money wage increases would decline as inflation decreased. In a similar manner, indexation would also remove the danger of firms being locked into excessively high nominal rates of interest. Contracts for loans would be fixed in real terms, and there would be no reason for firms to defer capital investment projects in anticipation of lower nominal rates of interest.

Two further points regarding indexation are appropriate. First, the implementation of indexation is not without cost, since scarce resources would be required to administer the system. It is a second-best solution since it would be better to have stable prices and no indexation. On the other hand, monetarists assert that control of inflation with indexation is less costly than either accelerating inflation or falling inflation accompanied by the higher level of unemployment that would occur without indexation. Second, there would be the potential danger that the introduction of indexation would cause an acceleration of inflation, if the original cause of inflation was due to sociological factors. This would not cause any anxiety to monetarists because of their belief (discussed in chapter 4) that inflation is always and everywhere a monetary phenomenon.

5.4.3 *Prices and incomes policies*

In a similar way to the above analysis, some monetarists believe that a prices and incomes policy may have a role to play as a short-run expedient to assist the transition to a lower rate of inflation by reducing inflationary expectations. Monetarists and Keynesians differ with regard to the length of time envisaged as necessary for such a policy. Some Keynesians tend to argue that a prices and incomes policy has a permanent role to play because of their belief in the role of sociological factors in the inflationary process. On the other hand, even those monetarists who believe that a prices and incomes policy has some role to play argue that this is only a temporary role. This role could also easily be frustrated if the government followed expansionary policies which created excess demand and which would be incompatible with price stability.

In the long run, monetarist analysis predicts that avoidance of excessive monetary expansion and therefore of excess demand is both a necessary and a sufficient condition to avoid inflation. However, both indexation and a prices and incomes policy (but particularly indexation) may have a role to play in the adjustment to a fixed rate of monetary growth.

5.5 Concluding remarks

The prescription to follow a rule is interlinked with the acceptance of the money supply as the target of policy. Permitting the money supply to grow at a constant rate is merely specifying the precise nature of the money supply target. The prescription is also closely related to the basic theoretical propositions of monetarism outlined in chapter 1. The beliefs (1) that the basic sources of short-run economic instability are monetary actions which result in accelerations and decelerations in the rate of growth of the money supply; (2) that monetary policy cannot peg the interest rate or the unemployment rate for more than very limited periods (see chapter 4) and (3) that the economy is inherently stable if not disturbed by erratic monetary growth suggest that monetary policy should not be used in a discretionary manner.

Although the acceptance of a monetary rule is closely interrelated with other basic monetarist views, it is possible to judge such a policy measure in isolation. If there was general agreement that discretionary monetary policy could be destabilising because of long and variable lags, many economists, including Keynesians, might support the adoption of a rule. On the other hand, one of the main reasons for the monetarists' preference for a monetary rule is the alleged lack of knowledge of the true relationship between money, income and prices. If this lack of knowledge could be remedied so that the relationship could be specified more precisely, many monetarists would probably reverse their preference for a monetary rule in favour of some discretionary policy. On this point Fand (1970) has argued that the contrasting views of monetarists and fiscalists concerning the rules discretion debate can be explained in terms of their historical development. He has suggested that the association of fiscalism with activism and discretion may reflect youthful enthusiasm, while that of monetarism with rules and guidelines may reflect middle-aged caution.

Monetarists argue that monetary policy, where the rate of growth of the money supply is governed by a rule, should replace fiscal policy as the main tool of economic stabilisation. In consequence this would leave fiscal policy to concentrate upon and return to its traditional roles (usurped by the Keynesian revolution) of influencing income distribution and resource allocation. In the next chapter we will discuss monetarist views on fiscal policy and the role fiscal policy can play in the economy.

Bibliography

*Titles marked * are particularly recommended for student reading.*

*Crockett, A. (1970), 'Timing Relationships Between Movements of Monetary and National Income Variables'. *Bank of England Quarterly Bulletin*, vol. 10 (December).

Culbertson, J. M. (1960), 'Friedman on the Lag in Effect of Monetary Policy'. *Journal of Political Economy*, vol. 68 (December).

Culbertson, J. M. (1961), 'The Lag in Effect of Monetary Policy: Reply'. *Journal of Political Economy*, vol. 69 (October).

Fand, D. (1970), 'Monetarism and Fiscalism'. *Banca Nazionale del Lavoro Quarterly Review*, no. 94 (September).

*Fisher, D. (1976), *Monetary Policy* (London: Macmillan).

Fischer, S. (1977), 'Long-Term Contracts, Rational Expectations, and the Optimal Money Supply Rule'. *Journal of Political Economy*, vol. 85 (February).

Friedman, B. (1975), 'Targets, Instruments and Indicators of Monetary Policy'. *Journal of Monetary Economics*, vol. 1.

Friedman, M. (1958), 'The Supply of Money and Changes in Prices and Output'. Reprinted in *The Optimum Quantity of Money and Other Essays* (Chicago: Aldine, 1969).

*Friedman, M. (1961), 'The Lag in the Effect of Monetary Policy'. *Journal of Political Economy*, vol. 69 (October). Reprinted in *The Optimum Quantity of Money and Other Essays* (Chicago: Aldine, 1969).

*Friedman, M. (1968), 'The Role of Monetary Policy'. *American Economic Review*, vol. 58 (March). Reprinted in *The Optimum Quantity of Money and Other Essays* (Chicago: Aldine, 1969).

Friedman, M. (1970), *The Counter-Revolution in Monetary Theory*. IEA Occasional Paper no. 33. (London: Institute of Economic Affairs.)

*Friedman, M. (1974), *Monetary Correction*. IEA Occasional Paper no. 41. (London: Institute of Economic Affairs.)

Kareken, J. and Solow, R. N. (1963), 'Monetary Policy: Lags versus Simultaneity'. *Commission on Money and Credit: Stabilization Policies.* (Englewood Cliffs, NJ: Prentice/Hall.)

*Laidler, D. E. W. (1971), 'The Phillips Curve, Expectations and Incomes Policy'. In H. G. Johnson and A. R. Nobay (eds), *The Current Inflation.* (London: Macmillan.)

*Laidler, D. E. W. (1973), 'Monetarist Policy Prescriptions and Their Background'. *The Manchester School* (March).

Mayer, T. (1975), 'The Structure of Monetarism'. *Kredit und Kapital*, vol. 8.

*Poole, W. (1970), 'Optimal Choice of Monetary Policy Instruments in a Simple Stochastic Macro Model'. *Quarterly Journal of Economics*, vol. 84 (May).

6 Fiscal Policy

In this chapter we will examine the role of fiscal policy in the light of the monetarist–Keynesian debate, but first of all it is desirable to define this term. Fiscal policy can be defined as any measure that alters the level, timing or composition of government expenditure and/or the level, timing or structure of tax payments. The relationship between government expenditure and tax revenue will be reflected in the position of the budget, which will be in surplus where tax revenue is greater than expenditure and in deficit where tax revenue is less than expenditure. An expansionary fiscal policy refers to an intended increase in the government budget deficit (reduced surplus), either through increased government expenditure or through reduced taxation. Conversely, a contractionary fiscal policy refers to an intended decrease in the budget deficit (increased surplus) by way of reduced expenditure or increased taxation. The qualification of intended policy measures is introduced to distinguish between planned policy changes and unplanned or automatic (i.e. endogenous) changes in the budget position arising from changes in tax yields or expenditure owing entirely to income changes.

It should be noted that our definition of budget deficits and surpluses excludes the considerable volume of lending to nationalised industries, local authorities and various other bodies which appears in the actual budget account. This type of expenditure, together with any related revenue, such as repayment of earlier debt, should be excluded from any measure of the strength of fiscal policy because, in this connection, the government's role is that of a financial intermediary transferring funds to ultimate borrowers.

Views concerning the power of fiscal policy to influence national income have changed dramatically from time to time, varying between the extremes of fiscal policy being impotent to that of it being very powerful. As one example of this change in view, we quote from Prime Minister J. Callaghan's speech to the 1976 UK Labour Party conference:

> We used to think that you could just spend your way out of a recession and increase employment by cutting taxes and boosting government spending. I tell you, in all candour, that that option no longer exists, and that, in so far as it ever did exist, it only worked by injecting bigger doses of inflation into the economy followed by higher levels of unemployment as the next step. That is the history of the past twenty years.

Throughout this chapter we shall be discussing the power of fiscal policy to influence real income and output. We shall therefore make the assumption that there is spare capacity in the economy so that

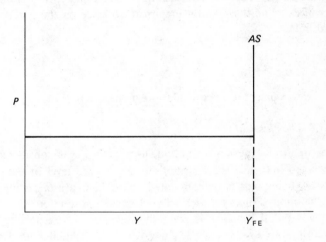

Figure 6.1

changes in aggregate demand induced by an expansionary fiscal policy produce changes in real output. If the economy is already at full employment, then quite clearly an expansionary fiscal policy will lead to a rising general price level. Equilibrium will then be established at a higher price level, so that real income will remain unchanged. The type of aggregate supply curve underlying this analysis is sometimes said to be reverse L-shaped because an increase in aggregate demand will result in either output changing at less than full employment or prices changing at full employment, but not both prices and output changing. The shape of this type of aggregate supply curve is shown in figure 6.1.

Initially, in section 6.1, we shall look at the development of the orthodox Keynesian view and subsequently, in section 6.2, we shall examine the rationale underlying the typical monetarist position that fiscal expansion will merely displace or crowd out an equivalent amount of private expenditure. In sections 6.3–6.5 we will discuss the effect that the introduction of the government budget constraint into the analysis has on the predictions of the power of fiscal policy. In view of the length of the discussion, we have subdivided this topic so that in 6.3 we will deal with the analysis within a closed economy, extending the analysis to the open economy in 6.4 before drawing the appropriate conclusions in 6.5. Finally, in section 6.6 we will examine the relevant empirical evidence on the potency of fiscal policy.

6.1 Development of the orthodox Keynesian view

6.1.1 *The classical view*

Prior to the Keynesian revolution, fiscal policy was considered to be able to influence the distribution but not the level of national income. This point is demonstrated below in figure 6.2 using the *IS–LM* model incorporating the classical assumption that the money demand function is perfectly inelastic with respect to the rate of interest so that the *LM* curve is vertical. Equilibrium occurs initially at Y_1 r_1. An expansionary fiscal policy will cause the *IS* curve to shift outwards to $IS(G_1)$ but, as long as the money supply remains unchanged, national income will not change. The only result is that the rate of interest will rise to r_2. The explanation for the failure of income to change is that the increase in the rate of interest will reduce private investment by an amount identical to the increase in government expenditure. This result is quite general, and a similar analysis (but in the reverse direction) will apply to increases in tax rates or to decreases in government expenditure. The

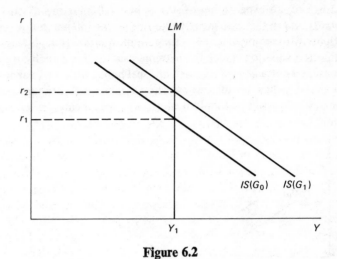

Figure 6.2

IS curve will shift inwards, lowering the rate of interest but leaving income unchanged because of an offsetting increase in private consumption owing to lower taxation and also in private investment following the reduction in interest rates. This general result is popularly known as the Treasury View.

6.1.2 *The horizontal* LM *curve*

However, with the Keynesian revolution, the role of interest rates in the money demand function became more heavily emphasised, and the assumption underlying a vertical *LM* curve was no longer considered justified. In fact, economic theorising tended to move to the other extreme of advocating a money demand function that exhibited almost perfect elasticity with respect to interest rate changes; and, while it is debatable how far Keynes himself accepted the existence of the liquidity trap (see e.g. Friedman, 1972), some Keynesians certainly tended to treat the liquidity trap as approximating the normal situation (see for example the Radcliffe Report, 1959, para. 391). This change in the analysis of the demand for money function and hence the slope of the *LM* curve produced a dramatic change in the prediction of the power of fiscal policy. This is shown in figure 6.3.

As before, an expansionary fiscal policy will shift the *IS* curve outwards, but in this case income will rise by the full amount of the multiplier without any change in the rate of interest. Thus, by highlighting the situation under the extreme case of the liquidity trap, Keynesians contrasted the strength of fiscal policy with the weakness of monetary policy, because, as was shown in section 2.2 (figure 2.3), monetary policy will be totally ineffective in influencing the level of output.

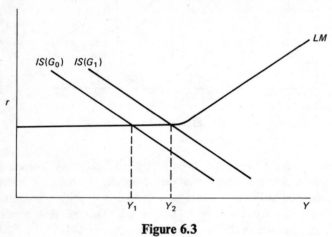

Figure 6.3

An alternative and perhaps more widely accepted reason for the existence of a horizontal *LM* curve arose from the assumption that the central bank pegged the rate of interest. As examined in section 3.4.3, this will cause the monetary base to become endogenous and the *LM* curve to become horizontal.

6.1.3   *A positive sloped* LM *curve*

This early Keynesian position was itself modified in the light of two developments. First, empirical evidence was accumulated suggesting that the elasticity of the demand for money was considerably less than the figure of infinity required for the existence of the liquidity trap, and second, doubts were raised concerning the stability of the marginal propensity to consume out of current income. The first development directed attention to the situation in which the *LM* curve is upward sloping, with the result that an expansionary fiscal policy will be only partially successful as the increase in income will be less than that predicted by the simple multiplier shown in figure 6.3. This is demonstrated in figure 6.4.

As before, an increase in government expenditure (or reduction in taxation) will cause the *IS* curve to shift outwards to $IS(G_1)$ but, instead of income rising to Y_3 (the prediction of the simple multiplier) it will increase only to Y_2. The reason why income will not increase by the full amount of the simple multiplier is that the rate of interest

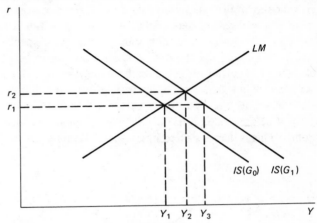

Figure 6.4

will rise from r_1 to r_2, thus reducing the level of private investment expenditure. Once the assumption of the liquidity trap had been abandoned, it became necessary to focus attention on how the increase in the government budget deficit (reduced surplus) was financed.

We will now refer back to the government budget constraint described in chapter 3, i.e.,

$$\Delta H \equiv PSD - OMO - NMD - BPF. \tag{6.1}$$

where (1) ΔH = change in high-powered money;
     (2) PSD = public sector deficit;
     (3) OMO = net open market sales of bonds;
     (4) NMD = sales of non-marketable debt;
     (5) BPF = finance available from balance of payments deficits.

Bond-financed fiscal expansion occurs where the public sector deficit and open market operations (or non-marketable debt) rise initially by equal amounts so that the change in high-powered money remains constant. On the other hand, fiscal expansion financed by high-powered money entails the public sector deficit and the change in high-powered money increasing initially by the same amounts, so that open market operations and sales of non-marketable debt are unchanged. In the case of bond finance only the *IS* curve will shift in the manner shown in figure 6.4. In contrast, if fiscal expansion is financed by selling reserve assets to the banking sector, this would cause the stock of high-powered money to increase (see appendix 1 to chapter 3). Assuming that there is a stable relationship between the stock of high-powered money and the money supply, this will lead to an increase in the money supply and a downward shift in the *LM* curve. Since both the *IS* and *LM* curves will shift, the increase in income will be greater than in the case where finance is raised by selling bonds. This is demonstrated in figure 6.5. Equilibrium occurs

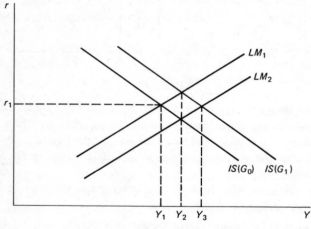

Figure 6.5

initially at $Y_1 r_1$. An expansionary fiscal policy will push the *IS* curve out to $IS(G_1)$ and in this case, because expansion is financed by an increase in high-powered money, the *LM* curve will also shift downwards from LM_1 to LM_2. Thus income will increase to Y_3, whereas if fiscal expansion is not accompanied by an increase in high-powered money income would only rise to Y_2.

6.1.4   *Government expenditure financed by taxes*

With regard to the second development, it is necessary to explain briefly the role of the multiplier in the Keynesian theory of fiscal policy. Increased budget deficits (reduced surpluses) were held to have a strong and predictable effect on the level of income because of the induced rise in consumption which itself would generate further increases in income. This is the familiar multiplier process with convergence to a new equilibrium level of income being assured because the marginal propensity to consume is less than one. However the development of the idea that consumption was a function not of current income but of long-run or average income, i.e. the permanent income or life-cycle hypotheses, suggested that the marginal propensity to consume out of current income would be quite small. As a result fiscal policy would alter consumption expenditure only to the extent that the private sector's assessment of their long-run income was altered. It was argued that, in fact, a single expansionary or contractionary change in fiscal policy would be likely to have only a small effect on the determination of long-run income.

One situation that is exempt from the above criticism is where an increase in government expenditure is financed by increased taxation so that the government budget deficit is unaltered. Under certain assumptions about the form of the tax, national income will rise by the full amount of the increase in government expenditure (i.e. the multiplier will equal 1). This result, known as the balanced-budget multiplier, is not dependent on changes in consumption following changes in taxation or government expenditure, and is therefore quite compatible with the view that consumption depends on long-run income. The adoption of more realistic assumptions (e.g. by including monetary effects; taxes and imports as functions of income) does nothing to destroy the basic thrust of the model, that income will rise if government expenditure and taxes are increased by the same amount. What is modified is the prediction that the rise in income will exactly equal the rise in government expenditure (i.e. that the balanced-budget multiplier will equal 1).

6.2   Fiscal policy and crowding out

6.2.1   *Nature of crowding out*

The typical monetarist view concerning fiscal policy is that pure fiscal expansion (i.e. without accommodating monetary expansion) may well exert some influence on national income in the short run, but that in the long run it will crowd out or replace some components of private expenditure so that real income remains unchanged. Crowding out will be complete if the reduction in private expenditure is identical in magnitude to the increase in government expenditure, so that the long-run fiscal multiplier will be 0. On the other hand, crowding out will be partial if income rises by an amount less than the increase in government expenditure, and in this case the value of the multiplier will be between 0 and 1. Absence of crowding out will be indicated by a fiscal multiplier of more than 1. In contrast, overcrowding out will exist where the fall in private expenditure is greater than the rise in government expenditure, in which case the multiplier will be negative.

The analysis of crowding out can be conducted in real or nominal terms. Crowding out in real terms refers to an offsetting reduction in real private expenditure, and, in the case of complete crowding out, for example, real national income and therefore employment remains unchanged in the long run. In contrast, complete crowding out in nominal terms means that nominal income remains unchanged following fiscal expansion. This is a far more restrictive concept than real crowding out, since if prices rise following fiscal expansion, then quantities (i.e. real income) must actually fall to leave nominal income unchanged.

Blinder and Solow (1973) have distinguished between the various levels at which crowding out may occur. However it should be noted that there appears to be no unified monetarist theme as to why crowding out should occur. The approach followed will be to present separately in the following sections instances in which crowding out may occur, noting these cases are not mutually exclusive.

6.2.2   *Direct replacement of private expenditure*

The first level at which crowding out may occur is where public sector investment is likely to replace private sector investment on a pound-for-pound basis. This will happen, for example, in the nationalised industries where nationalisation entails the public sector instead of the private sector investing in the same capital projects. The only reason for advocating the existence of a discrepancy between these two sources of expenditure would arise from a political rather than an economic stance, i.e. that the public sector is less or more efficient than the private sector in perceiving and subsequently administering investment projects. As a consequence, views on this facet of crowding out are wide-ranging. There are those who argue that the level of public expenditure can be varied, both spatially and over time, to offset deficiencies in private expenditure, thus increasing total output*. On the other hand, some economists argue that this type of government expenditure is inherently wasteful, so that 'these enterprises direct material, skilled labour and capital towards less productive uses than the private output which is crowded out' (Brunner and Meltzer, 1976). This aspect of the debate cannot be resolved in a strictly economic framework and is, therefore, not pursued further in this chapter. For the rest of this chapter, we shall concentrate on the controversy surrounding the so-called non-productive government expenditure (e.g. defence, social projects such as new hospitals etc.).

6.2.3 *The effect of changes in interest rates*

The second level at which crowding out may arise is in the case of bond finance where the *LM* curve is not horizontal. This situation has already been discussed in section 6.1.3 (figure 6.4), where it was demonstrated that an increase in government expenditure financed by an increase in bonds will cause the rate of interest to rise. This will cause a reduction in private sector investment and, therefore, a reduction in the growth of the capacity of the economy. If the *LM* curve is not vertical, crowding out at this level cannot be complete. Monetarists accept that the *LM* curve is not vertical (see e.g. Friedman, 1972) and do not use this extreme case as the justification for their belief in crowding out. However Friedman (1976) has

---

* It is worth noting that, both in the *General Theory* and subsequently in *The Times*, Keynes stressed the importance of the composition of public sector and private sector expenditure respectively. If government spending could be directed to the output of industries with a relatively high elasticity of production, then, it is argued, there would be little short-run damage to private sector production.

pointed out that, even within the confines of a simple *IS–LM* model in which the slopes of the two curves are used to assess the potential power of policy measures, the vertical *LM* curve is not the only extreme case in which fiscal policy will be impotent. Similar results will be obtained if the *IS* curve is horizontal. As can be seen from figure 6.6 below, fiscal expansion cannot, in this case, alter the rate of interest because an infinitesimally small change in the rate of interest will produce a change in investment equal in magnitude but opposite in sign to the fiscal expansion. In this case fiscal changes

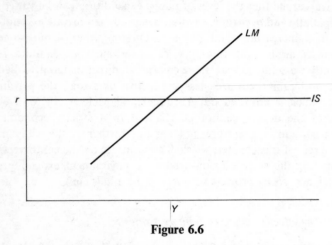

Figure 6.6

are unable to alter the position of the *IS* curve and therefore crowding out will be complete in both real and nominal terms.

The rationale behind this concept of a horizontal *IS* curve is attributed to the writings of Frank Knight (see Carlson and Spencer, 1975, and also Friedman, 1976) and is based on the idea that diminishing returns should not accrue to new investment. One reason for the absence of diminishing returns is the large size of existing capital stock relative to that of investment, so that additions to this stock should not alter to any significant extent the yield on capital. A second reason is that improved technology is associated with new investment and this should offset any tendency towards diminishing returns.

In a series of articles in the *Journal of Political Economy* Friedman (1971b, 1972) has argued that the terms 'investment' and 'saving' have to be defined more broadly than the normal interpretation afforded to them by Keynesians. This view implies that a change in interest rates will affect a much broader category of expenditure than business investment in fixed capital and inventories together with housing construction. Hence the *IS* curve will be flatter than normally drawn (tending to be horizontal as in the Knight case), and this will reduce the impact of the direct effect of fiscal expansion given a positive sloped *LM* curve.

Friedman (1972) has also argued that government securities are close substitutes for private securities in portfolios. Increased sales of government bonds will lead to a significant reduction in the sale of private bonds and, therefore, in the quantity of finance available to private firms. In other words, private securities would be crowded out of portfolios and replaced by government securities. As Brunner and Meltzer (1976) have pointed out, this is another facet of the rise in interest rates described earlier. The overall result will be a fall in the level of private investment and a lower rate of growth of economic capacity. Crowding out will, therefore, occur over time.

The third and more important level at which crowding out may occur depends on the reactions of economic agents to the changes brought about by fiscal expansion. In particular, two such variables have been considered important: confidence in the economic future, and private sector wealth. In the following sections we shall discuss the relevance of these two factors to the crowding-out debate.

6.2.4 *Confidence and crowding out*

An expansionary fiscal policy might affect expectations regarding the future. If, for example, the private sector's confidence in the economic future is adversely affected by the budget deficit, liquidity preference (i.e. the demand for money) could increase, leading to a backward shift in the *LM* curve. At the same time, lack of confidence in the future could cause the business community to lower their estimates of future returns from new investment projects, i.e., the marginal efficiency of capital would fall. This will cause the investment schedule to decrease and the *IS* curve to shift inwards. This is demonstrated in figure 6.7. An increase in government expenditure from G_0 to G_1 will cause the *IS* curve to shift outwards from $IS(G_0)$ to $IS(G_1)$ and the equilibrium level of income to rise from Y_1 to Y_2. The change in the private sector's confidence will however cause the

IS curve to move inwards and the *LM* curve to move upwards. Equilibrium will be re-established at a level of income below Y_2. If crowding out is complete income would return to Y_1. If however crowding out is partial, the equilibrium level of income would be between Y_1 and Y_2.

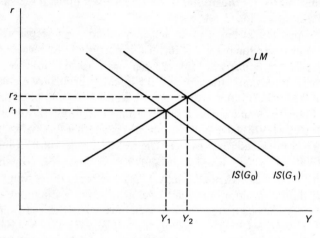

Figure 6.7

Other views on crowding out depend on a relationship between wealth and on both private expenditure and the demand for money. Before examining these relationships, we will discuss the nature of wealth.

6.2.5   *The nature of wealth*

For the individual economic unit, total wealth can be broadly defined as the stock of assets held by that unit. A wide variety of assets would be considered to be wealth in terms of this definition, but it is convenient to subdivide these assets into three broad categories: (1) real capital, (2) money (however defined), and (3) financial securities. Net wealth can be defined as total wealth less outstanding liabilities. Therefore in deriving the net wealth of the economy, it is usual to set assets against liabilities. Financial assets are assets to their holders but liabilities to those bodies/individuals who issued them. These will, therefore, cancel each other out in the measurement of net wealth. This is known as consolidating balance sheets and is applicable in this context to financial assets and money. In addition, the problem of double-counting needs to be avoided. For example, equity capital involves ownership of physical capital, and the inclusion in net wealth of both share capital and physical capital owned by companies would be an example of double-counting.

When discussing the influence of net wealth on expenditure, a distinction is often made between the private and the public sectors. With regard to the private sector, it is argued that expenditure will be influenced by their stocks of both assets and liabilities, so that it is legitimate to net out such items in the measurement of the relevant concept of wealth. In contrast, government expenditure is dependent on political factors and the general state of the economy. It is therefore argued that the volume of government expenditure will not be influenced by the level of its outstanding liabilities. It follows that a distinction should be made between the private and the public sectors when net wealth is being measured: private sector assets and liabilities should be netted out, but private sector holdings of public sector liabilities should be included as a component of net wealth.

Similar arguments can be made with regard to the problem of how far money should be considered a component of net wealth. As discussed in chapter 3, deposits can be created by the banks either through making loans or through purchasing financial securities. Thus in terms of their balance sheets, deposits are the liabilities of the banks, and their holdings of financial securities plus loans are their assets. Therefore, consolidating the balance of sheets of the banking sector with the non-bank private sector would produce a zero component of net wealth. This abstracts from (a) the banks' financial reserves and real assets and (b) their holdings of government debt.

In connection with the liabilities of the public sector, a distinction is made between (a) outside money and (b) inside money. Outside money can be defined as notes and coins held by the non-bank public plus bank deposits created through the purchase by the banks of public sector debt. In contrast, inside money is created by lending to the private sector. In the case of inside money, bank deposits and private debt to the banks will cancel each other out in the measurement of net wealth. However in the case of outside money, there will be no such cancellation because the matching liabilities are government debt.

Net non-human wealth of the private sector can therefore be defined
in money terms by the following identity (in order to facilitate the
exposition of this analysis, we ignore the effects of changes in interest
rates on bond prices):

$$W \equiv PK + M_0 + B \qquad (6.2)$$

where (1) P = the price level;
   (2) K = existing real stock of capital;
   (3) M_0 = outside money;
   (4) B = government bonds (other than those appearing in
               M_0).

The above definition of wealth is widely used but is not one that
is universally acceptable. For example, Pesek and Saving (1967) have
advocated the inclusion of the total money supply rather than just
outside money on the grounds that bank deposits are assets produced
by banks and sold to the public. Similarly, Brunner (1971) has
suggested that the outside money component should be multiplied
by a factor greater than 1 so as to incorporate the capitalised value
of the net earnings of the banking sector. An additional complication,
discussed later in this section, is that it has sometimes been argued
that bonds should be excluded from the definition of wealth on
grounds of rationality (see e.g. Barro, 1974). The basis of this view
is that the private sector would realise that increased bond issues
would necessitate increases in taxes in the future to meet interest
payments on and redemption of the bonds. These future tax
liabilities would be discounted and would appear as a negative item
in the measurement of net wealth. While every owner regards his
bonds as net wealth to him, this is offset by others who regard the
discounted value of the necessary extra taxes as reducing the value
of their wealth to them.

Generally we shall use identity (6.2) to define private sector wealth.
It should also be noted that price increases will reduce real wealth,
ceteris paribus, since both outside money and bonds are denominated
in nominal terms.

6.2.6   *Wealth and crowding out*

Wealth will exert a positive influence on both the quantity of money
demanded and on consumption expenditure. Increases in wealth

will, therefore, lead to increases in the quantity of money demanded and consumption expenditure. Fiscal expansion, financed by increased bond issues, will lead to an increase in private wealth (owing to the increased bond holdings) and hence to an increase in private consumption expenditure. This will, in its turn, reinforce the impact effect of fiscal expansion on aggregate demand causing a further outward shift of the *IS* curve. Even in the short run this is not the end of the story. The increase in private wealth will also increase the demand for money, which will cause the *LM* curve to shift upwards. Whether income expands or contracts will depend on the relative shifts of the two curves, and therefore on the sensitivity of money demand and that of consumption expenditure to changes in wealth.

In the long run increases in the general price level will occur if sufficient unemployed resources are not available to produce the extra goods demanded. This will cause a decrease in the real value of the supply of money and wealth fixed in nominal terms. As the private sector sells bonds to restore the real value of their nominal money holdings, the rate of interest will rise, and at the same time, owing to the fall in the value of outside money, consumption will decrease. In other words, the *IS* curve will shift inwards and the *LM* curve will shift upwards. This is demonstrated in figure 6.8. Fiscal expansion will raise income from Y_1 to Y_2 and complete crowding out would occur if the *LM* curve shifted upwards and/or the *IS*

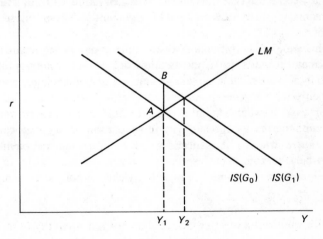

Figure 6.8

curve shifted inwards so that, in the long run, income returned to Y_1 with the curves intersecting between points A and B on the line indicating an output level of Y_1. Clearly, crowding out under this heading will be larger, (a) the more responsive prices are to fiscal expansion and (b) the more responsive private expenditure (in real terms) is to increases in the general price level. If the public (i.e. consumers and/or producers) expect prices to rise following fiscal expansion, then the more likely it is that prices will respond quickly and significantly so that crowding out will occur (see sections 4.4.2 and 4.4.3 for a discussion of the role of price expectations in inflation). If, on the other hand, the public expects the price level to remain constant (e.g. after a long period of stable prices), prices will not be particularly responsive to fiscal expansion so that crowding out from this source would be minimal. It is difficult to argue that, in the conditions of the 1970s, the public would expect the price level to remain constant following fiscal expansion. If this is a correct representation of the prevailing situation, then prices would be very responsive to fiscal expansion and crowding out from this source would be potentially significant.

It was noted above that consumption will rise owing to the increase in wealth when fiscal expansion is financed by the sale of bonds and that this indirect effect will reinforce the direct effects of fiscal expansion on aggregate demand. Friedman (1972) has argued that these indirect effects will be substantially reduced because the public will realise that the increased issue of bonds will entail future increases in taxes (the rationality argument discussed in section 6.2.5).

This view of the rationality of the public may be objected to on two main grounds. First, the assumed degree of foresight is unreal and, in any case, the transfers arising out of bond finance may be not only within generations but also between generations. In this latter case it would be irrational for the present generation to discount the tax liabilities of future generations. Second, it can be questioned whether it is necessary that future interest payments must be met from taxes, especially if unemployment exists. In this case increases in income will raise tax yields without any change in tax rates.

6.2.7   *Crowding out in the open economy*

So far the discussion has taken place within the confines of a self-contained economy. However in an open economy a further source of potential crowding out arises in respect of the behaviour of exports and imports following fiscal expansion. If prices rise after fiscal expansion and the exchange rate is fixed, exports will become less competitive with foreign goods, whereas imports will become more competitive with domestically produced goods. Thus exports would decrease and imports increase causing the *IS* curve to shift inwards.

6.3   Closed economy: the government budget constraint

6.3.1   *The nature of the government budget constraint*

Up to now the analysis has largely ignored the link between fiscal and monetary policy (i.e. the effect of the public sector deficit on high-powered money discussed in chapter 3). The effect of incorporating a government budget constraint into the standard *IS–LM* model was first examined by Ott and Ott (1965) and by Christ (1968), but perhaps the main impetus to the discussion of this development came from Blinder and Solow (1973). The literature is comprehensively surveyed in Currie (1977).

The central proposition in this analysis is that long-run equilibrium in a macroeconomic model requires stock equilibrium in addition to flow equilibrium. The crucial distinction between stocks and flows is that a flow (e.g. income or investment) has a value over a period of time (e.g. per month or per year), whereas a stock is an asset (e.g. wealth or capital stock) that has a value at a point of time. Therefore in the context of an economy that is not growing over time, the supply of financial assets cannot be changing, otherwise stock equilibrium would be disturbed. Hence, assuming a self-contained economy, long-run equilibrium is not possible if there is a budget deficit because, in order to finance the deficit, the authorities would have to issue either bonds or money so that the supply of financial assets would change. Similarly, the assumption of constant wealth also requires both net saving and net investment to be equal to zero, otherwise private sector wealth would change.

In the analysis that follows we shall assume that the economy is not growing over time and therefore that the existence of both a balanced government budget and zero net saving (and also net investment) are necessary for long-run static equilibrium. These are rather unreal assumptions and are adopted for ease of exposition. In section 6.5 we shall review briefly the analysis based on the alternative assumption that the economy attains an equilibrium growth path.

The introduction of the government budget constraint and the requirement of stock equilibrium into the standard *IS–LM* model affects the credibility of the typical monetarist view that fiscal policy is impotent. In the following sections this particular aspect of the debate will be considered.

6.3.2 *The government budget constraint and wealth*

Identities (6.1) and (6.2) describe the budget constraint and the definition of wealth and are reproduced below:

$$\Delta H \equiv PSD - OMO - NMD - BPF. \tag{6.1}$$

$$W \equiv PK + M_o + B. \tag{6.2}$$

Since we are assuming a closed economy, the last term in identity (6.1) is irrelevant, so that (6.1) becomes

$$\Delta H \equiv PSD - OMO - NMD. \tag{6.3}$$

It is apparent from these two identities that government expenditure, whether financed by sales of bonds or by an increase in high-powered money, will change the total of private sector wealth. This change in wealth owing to the increased private sector holdings of government bonds or money would be expected to increase private sector expenditure and the quantity of money demanded. The only way that these effects could be ignored would be to assume that private sector expenditure is not influenced by its wealth holdings and that either there are no wealth effects in the money demand function or that government expenditure is financed by an appropriate combination of bonds and high-powered money so as to leave the position of the *LM* curve unchanged. This will occur when the increases in money and bonds exactly match the increased demands for these assets arising out of the increases in wealth. The assumption of the absence of wealth effects seems unreal in both theory and practice, whereas that of the government being able to issue bonds and high-powered money in the appropriate proportions (such that the position of the *LM* curve remains unchanged) seems unreal in practice. The consequence of incorporating the government budget constraint into the *IS–LM* model is to demonstrate that long-run equilibrium requires a balanced government budget. In the following pages we shall examine the effect that this requirement has on the analysis of the impact of fiscal policy.

6.3.3 *The government budget constraint and fiscal policy*

Initially we shall concentrate on the standard Keynesian under-employment model with fixed prices. Starting from a position of long-run full stock equilibrium, and also abstracting from private sector investment and saving an increase in government expenditure, would raise national income. Initially, however, this would cause a government budget deficit and stock equilibrium would be disturbed. The re-establishment of full stock equilibrium would require increases in national income such that government tax revenue equals the increased government expenditure.

This analysis is shown in figure 6.9. The top panel depicts the normal *IS–LM* model and the lower panel shows government expenditure and revenue through taxes. Government expenditure *GG* is assumed to be invariant to changes in income, which means that either there are no welfare payments or alternatively that the tax function *TT* is shown net of such payments (i.e. they are deducted from tax revenue). The slope of the tax function represents the marginal rate of tax, assumed to be constant in this case, and the distance *OT* the level of income necessary before any tax will be paid. In this figure positive values occur on either side of the horizontal axis, i.e. positive rates of interest upwards and positive values of government expenditure and taxes downwards. Income level Y_1 represents long-run equilibrium with a balanced government budget and also zero net saving and net investment.

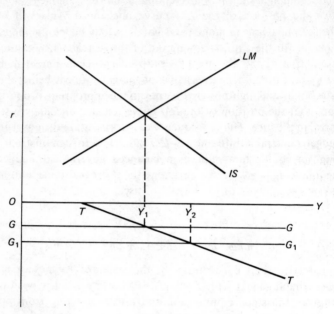

Figure 6.9

An increase in government expenditure will cause the *IS* curve to shift outwards and the government expenditure function to shift downwards from GG to G_1G_1. To be in a long-run equilibrium situation income would have to rise to Y_2, closing the budget deficit; or, in terms of the government budget constraint (i.e. identity 6.2), long-run equilibrium is possible only in a closed economy, where

$$\Delta H = PSD = OMO = NMD = 0. \tag{6.4}$$

It is against this background that we will now discuss the impact of the wealth effects. As was mentioned earlier, these will cause the *IS* curve to shift outwards and the *LM* curve to shift upwards. If we assume that the wealth effect on private expenditure is stronger than that on the demand for money, the continual shifts of the *IS* curves following the increased private sector bond holdings owing to the budget deficit will be larger than the upward shifts of the *LM* curve. Thus long-run equilibrium will be re-established when the budget is balanced and private sector wealth is again constant, i.e. at an income level of Y_2.

It is interesting to note that in the case where an increase in government expenditure is financed by an increase in high-powered money, the *LM* curve will shift downwards, but that the condition for long-run equilibrium will still necessitate income rising to Y_2. In this case there will be continual shifts of the *LM* curve as high-powered money is increased until such time as the budget deficit is eliminated. We have then the interesting and surprising result that the government expenditure multiplier will be the same whether financed by selling bonds or financed by increasing the stock of high-powered money. The multiplier will be equal to the reciprocal of the marginal tax rate.

However, stability is not automatically ensured in any macro-economic model. In this context consider what will happen where the shifts of the *LM* curve, induced by increases in wealth arising out of the increased private sector bond holdings owing to the budget deficit, are larger than the wealth-induced shifts of the *IS* curve. In this instance the equilibrium level of income will continually decrease and the budget deficit will become larger because as income falls tax receipts will fall, given the rate of tax. In other words, since income will be continually driven further away from its equilibrium level (Y_2 in figure 6.9), there will be instability in the model, and in practice this will mean that the fiscal expansion will be reversed. Incidentally, it is just possible, but unlikely, that the wealth-induced shift of the *IS* curve will exactly offset that of the *LM* curve, and in this case long-run equilibrium with a balanced budget will never be attained, but on the other hand income will not fall continually, i.e., the model will not be unstable.

How then does this analysis affect the monetarist–Keynesian debate and, in particular, the probability of crowding out discussed in the previous section? In the case of fiscal expansion financed by bond sales, if the model is stable with wealth-induced effects on the *IS* curve being stronger than those on the *LM* curve, then crowding out will be absent. On the other hand, if crowding out is present and the wealth-induced shifts of the *LM* curve are greater than those of the *IS* curve, then instability will result. Income will fall continually; i.e., complete crowding out in a stable model is not possible given the assumption of underemployment equilibrium and therefore a constant price level.

6.3.4   *The budget constraint and fiscal policy: a change of definition*

The results discussed in section 6.3.3 depend on a definition of government expenditure that includes interest payments on outstanding government bonds. In this case, holding government expenditure constant necessitates reducing other components of government expenditure in order to offset rising interest payments in the case of bond finance. An alternative assumption, which is in fact the one used by Blinder and Solow (1973), is that government expenditure is defined to exclude interest payments on bonds. In the case of bond finance, rising total interest payments on the increased bond issues will mean that total government expenditure (i.e. including interest payments) will continue to increase (i.e. the line GG in figure 6.9 shifting downwards) until the budget is balanced. The final equilibrium level of income would then be to the right of Y_2. If the method of finance is by increasing the quantity of high-powered money, there would be no further increase in total government expenditure, assuming no interest payments are made on high-powered money. The equilibrium level of income would then be at Y_2. Thus we arrive at the paradoxical result that the government expenditure multiplier will be greater in the case of bond finance than that of monetary expansion.

6.3.5   *The variable price case*

A major criticism of the foregoing analysis is that it is conducted in terms of a constant price level and excludes by definition many of the crowding-out effects discussed in section 6.2. The assumption of a constant price level is one that monetarists would argue is unrealistic. In the following section, therefore, we shall relax the assumption of constant prices, noting that with rising prices long-run equilibrium no longer requires a balanced budget.

For ease of exposition it is convenient to assume that the equilibrium occurs initially with a zero rate of inflation and a balanced budget. We shall also assume that (a) inflation is possible only if there is excess demand and (b) that there is a natural rate of unemployment consistent with a zero rate of inflation (or, for that matter, with any constant rate of inflation). As discussed in chapter 4, unemployment can be maintained below this natural rate only at the cost of ever-increasing rates of inflation. In the case of government expenditure financed by bond issues, inflation will occur as output increases and unemployment falls below the natural rate. A new and stable equilibrium will be possible only if real income rises sufficiently to close the budget deficit. Elimination of the budget deficit will occur only if the natural rate of unemployment falls and/or productivity increases so that real income rises. If neither of these possibilities occurs, real income cannot rise and the budget deficit will not be eliminated. The result will therefore be instability with decreasing income or increasing rates of inflation, depending on whether the increase in wealth has a stronger effect on money demand or on private expenditure. This contrasts with the case of an increase in government expenditure financed by an expansion of high-powered money. Equilibrium could occur with the resulting increase in the money supply matching the increased demand for money arising out of an increase in nominal income induced by inflation. Even in this case some bond finance would be necessary to maintain the private sector's demand for bonds in equilibrium as well as its demand for money.

One qualification to this analysis is appropriate. If tax rates are progressive and are not altered by the government in response to inflation, the budget could be balanced without real income increasing because inflation will push the average tax yield up through fiscal drag. In this case it is possible but not certain that stability could result with, at the same time, fiscal policy crowding out private expenditure.

6.3.6 *Bonds and net wealth*

An objection to all these conclusions (i.e. those based on the inclusion of the budget constraint in the model) can be made on the grounds of rationality. As has been argued earlier in this chapter (section 6.2.5), the private sector may realise that the increased issues of bonds will mean future increases in taxes to meet interest payments on and redemption of these bonds. These future payments would then be discounted and their present value would be perceived to offset the rise in wealth arising from increased private sector bond holdings. On the assumption of a perfect capital market, there would be no increase in wealth following bond-financed government expenditure and, therefore, no wealth-induced shifts in the *IS* or *LM* curves. There would then be no need for the government budget to be balanced and the problem of instability would not arise. The impact of government expenditure would be the same whether financed by taxes or by bond sales.

However, with the assumption of rationality, government expenditure financed by increases in high-powered money will be more expansionary (the *IS* curve shifts outwards and *LM* curve downwards) than when finance is raised either by bond issues or taxes (only the *IS* curve moves). This view is in accordance with the traditional Keynesian ranking of the various types of fiscal policy with regard to their power.

As has been indicated earlier in section 6.2.6, objections can be raised against this rationality argument on the grounds that the private sector lacks the necessary degree of foresight and also that real income might rise, causing tax revenue to increase, thus obviating the need for future tax increases. Furthermore, the absence of wealth effects because of the exclusion of government bonds from the definition of private sector wealth on the grounds of rationality requires the very strong belief that the discounted value of the future tax payments necessary to meet future interest payments on and redemption of the bonds exactly offsets the value of the bond holdings. A more general definition of wealth would be

$$W = PK + \alpha M_0 + \lambda B; \quad 0 \leqslant \alpha \lambda \leqslant 1; \tag{6.6}$$

where α and λ are the fractions of outside money and government bonds regarded by the private sector as net wealth.

This amendment to the wealth identity (apart, that is, from the extreme case where α and λ equal zero) would reduce the magnitude of the wealth effects examined in this chapter and consequently lengthen the time necessary for long-run stock equilibrium to be attained, but would not remove the requirement that the government budget must be balanced if long-run stock equilibrium is to be achieved.

6.4   The open economy: the government budget constraint

If we now relax the assumption of a closed economy and turn to an open economy with a regime of fixed exchange rates, then the balance of payments acts in a similar way to the government budget constraint in a closed economy. For example, a balance of payments deficit (i.e. on the combined total of the capital and current accounts) decreases, *ceteris paribus*, the supply of high-powered money, as can be seen from the government budget identity (6.1):

$$\Delta H \equiv PSD - OMO - NMD - BPF \tag{6.1}$$

The important conclusion is that, unlike the case of the closed economy, long-run equilibrium does not require the government budget to be balanced. Open market operations can sum to zero so that wealth remains unchanged with a non-zero public sector deficit as long as the balance of payments deficit is of an identical magnitude.

It is of course true that the existence of the balance of payments deficit will cause the country's holdings of foreign exchange reserves to fall and that, therefore, the duration of time that the deficit can be sustained will depend on the level of the country's foreign exchange reserves. Nevertheless, it is equally true that the movement of the economy away from the equilibrium where the balance of payments deficit exactly matches the government budget deficit is not automatic but requires a deliberate act of policy. This link between the balance of payments and high-powered money, the so-called Monetary Approach to the Balance of Payments, is examined in more detail in chapter 7.

Unfortunately, the extension of the model to the open economy renders the analysis more complicated and also makes the predictions ambiguous with regard to the long-run impact of fiscal policy on income and output.

6.4.1   *Extension of the model to the open economy*

The extension of the standard *IS–LM* analysis to incorporate the balance of payments is illustrated in figure 6.10 where the *IS* and *LM* curves are derived in the normal manner with the inclusion of net exports (exports—imports) as a component of aggregate demand. *BP* represents a balance of payments function showing combinations of interest rates and income levels that yield a zero balance on the sum of the capital and current accounts. This function will have a positive slope because, as income increases, net exports will decrease (assuming imports are a positive function of income), thus requiring a higher rate of interest to induce the increased capital net inflow

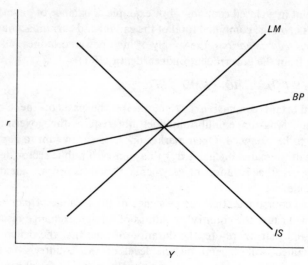

Figure 6.10

necessary to maintain a zero balance of payments. The derivation of the *BP* curve takes into consideration interest payments on increased borrowings from abroad. With fixed exchange rates, a payments surplus occurs where the *IS–LM* intersection is above the *BP* curve, since the rate of interest is higher (and therefore the capital inflow greater) than that necessary to produce a zero balance of payments given the level of income. Conversely, any point of intersection below the *BP* line represents a balance of payments deficit, since the interest rate is lower than that necessary to attain a zero balance of payments. In figure 6.10 the *BP* function represents a situation of imperfect capital mobility since the domestic rate of interest can depart from that ruling in the rest of the world. Perfect capital mobility would be represented by a horizontal *BP* curve with the relevant rate of interest equal to that ruling in the rest of the world. The other extreme case, i.e. zero capital mobility, would be represented by a vertical *BP* curve at the level of income at which the sum of net exports and the exogenous capital flow equals zero. In the analysis that follows we shall concentrate on the situation in which imperfect capital mobility exists and the price level remains constant.

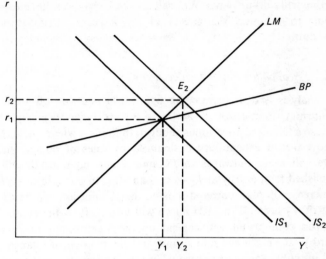

Figure 6.11

The next step in the analysis is to examine how these curves shift in response to changes in relevant variables – apart, that is, from the wealth effects on the *IS* and *LM* curves already discussed in this chapter. We shall now consider an appreciation of the exchange rate. In this connection the relative price of domestic to foreign goods can be defined as:

$$\frac{eP}{P_w}$$

where P is the domestic price level in terms of domestic currency; e is the exchange rate expressing domestic currency in terms of foreign currency (i.e. £ in terms of $ e.g. in mid-1977 approximately $1.70); and P_w is the world price level in terms of foreign currency. An appreciation of the exchange rate (increasing e) will make domestic goods less competitive with foreign goods and will therefore reduce the volume of net exports for each level of income. Since net exports are a component of aggregate demand, the *IS* curve will shift inwards. The reduction in net exports will also require a greater capital inflow to attain a zero balance of payments for each level of income and hence a higher rate of interest. Thus the *BP* function will shift upwards. We shall use these results in the following section to examine the effects of an increase in government expenditure.

6.4.2   *Fiscal policy in the open economy*

The analysis is demonstrated in figure 6.11, starting off from an equilibrium situation of Y_1 and r_1 with zero balance of payments and also a balanced government budget. In the case where an increase in government expenditure is financed by sales of bonds, the IS curve will move outwards to IS_2 and a new equilibrium will be established temporarily at E_2 with r_2 and Y_2. In the case of finance by increases in high-powered money, the equilibrium will be to the right of Y_2 because the LM curve will also shift to the right. The long-run equilibrium will depend on the assumptions made with regard to the exchange rate regime and the method of finance. We shall initially examine the case where the budget deficit is financed by an increase in high-powered money against a background of both fixed exchange rates and also floating exchange rates. Subsequently we shall look at the case of bond finance within the two exchange rate regimes.

The initial equilibrium with fixed exchange rates where the government expenditure is financed by an increase in high-powered money implies a government budget deficit (requiring further increases in the money supply) and a balance of payments surplus. The increases in the money supply owing to the budget deficit and balance of payments surplus will cause the LM curve to shift downwards. The IS curve will also shift to the right, owing to an increase in private sector wealth following the increase in outside (high-powered) money. Long-run equilibrium will occur either with both the balance of payments and government budget identically equal to zero, or with a government budget deficit equal in magnitude to the balance of payments deficit. Either situation is compatible with zero expansion of high-powered money and therefore with full stock equilibrium of the private sector. Which of the two situations prevails will depend on the speed with which the government budget deficit is eliminated relative to that with which the balance of payments moves from surplus to deficit.

In the case of floating exchange rates (which entails by definition a zero balance of payments), the initial equilibrium implies an appreciation of the exchange rate which will cause the *IS* curve to shift inwards. In this case the *BP* curve will also shift upwards owing to exchange rate appreciation. However, despite the contractionary effect induced by the shifts of the *IS* and *BP* curves, long-run equilibrium can occur only with a balanced government budget because the money supply will continue to increase while the government budget is in deficit. This implies that fiscal expansion financed by changes in high-powered money will be at least as powerful with floating exchange rates as with fixed exchange rates. In fact, it is likely to be more expansionary, since with floating exchange rates long-run full stock equilibrium will be possible only when income rises to a level sufficient to balance the budget. In contrast, with fixed exchange rates long-run full stock equilibrium could occur at a lower level of income provided the resulting budget deficit is matched by a balance of payments deficit of identical magnitude.

In contrast to money finance, bond finance is likely to be unstable. In figure 6.11, equilibrium E_2 implies a budget deficit financed by bond issues. In the case of fixed exchange rates, further issues of bonds will be required to finance this deficit. Thus the *IS* curve will shift to the right (assuming that the increased bond holdings by the private sector, arising out of the budget deficit, are greater than the loss owing to the capital inflow) and the *LM* curve will shift upwards. As in the closed economy case, stability will only occur if the wealth effect on aggregate demand is greater than that on money demand, so that equilibrium will be established at a higher level of income. This can occur with either a balanced government budget and a zero balance of payments or with a government budget deficit matched by a balance of payments deficit. In the case of the floating exchange rate stability is less likely, since the appreciation of the exchange rate will be a force pushing the *IS* curve to the left and offsetting, at least partially, the expansionary wealth effect on aggregate demand.

6.5 The government budget constraint: conclusions

In the two preceding sections we have examined what effect the introduction of the government budget constraint (together with wealth effects on private expenditure and money demand) will have on the analysis of the potency of fiscal policy. With traditional Keynesian assumptions of stable prices, underemployment equilibrium and a closed economy, the monetarist prediction that fiscal policy is impotent is open to criticism that the analysis predicts either instability or a powerful role for fiscal policy in determining real income and output in the long run. Removing these assumptions however renders the analysis more ambiguous, and, in fact, Blinder and Solow (1976) have argued that a bond-financed government deficit will have a significant impact on real income in the short run but that in the long run the effect on real income will be 'completely dissipated' if the long-run Phillips curve is vertical. If the Phillips curve is not vertical there will be a 'small positive effect on real output'.

In section 6.3.1 we stated that we would briefly review the analysis based on the alternative assumption that the economy is growing over time. The growth path of such an economy would be considered to be an equilibrium growth path if there was no tendency for the economy to move away from that growth path. It would also be considered to be stable provided that the actual growth path of the economy moved back to the equilibrium path whenever a divergence occurred. For such a growing economy, wealth would be increasing because net investment and net saving would no longer be zero. There would therefore be a positive incremental demand for both bonds and money. Hence, to the extent that the resulting issues of bonds and high-powered money met this demand, there would be no need for the government budget to be balanced.

The permissible size of the budget deficit would be, however, tightly constrained by (a) the growth of wealth and (b) the elasticity of demand of both bonds and money with respect to wealth. If fiscal expansion resulted in a budget deficit larger than the permitted size, then the effects would be similar to those analysed in sections 6.3 and 6.4 for the static economy. We see therefore no reason to modify significantly the general conclusions of the analysis of the static economy.

6.6 Empirical evidence

In view of the ambiguous nature of the *a priori* predictions regarding the potency of fiscal policy, one possible way of resolving the argument is to look at the empirical evidence. In principle two types of evidence are available: single-equation estimates, and the simulation of macroeconomic models.

6.6.1 *Single-equation estimates*

Single-equation estimates are of the general form:

$$Y = f(M; F) \tag{6.7}$$

$$\Delta Y = f(\Delta M; \Delta F) \tag{6.8}$$

where Y = income or output, M = money supply or high-powered money and F = some measure of fiscal influence. This type of equation is the reduced form (i.e. solution of the endogenous variables in terms of the exogenous variables) of an unspecified model of the economy.

The seminal study comparing the potency of fiscal and monetary policy was that carried out by Andersen and Jordan (1968) on US data for the period 1952–68. A summary of their findings is presented below.

(1) The estimated co-efficient for the monetary variable was found to be highly significant statistically with the correct sign (i.e. positive).

(2) The estimated coefficient for the fiscal variable (defined as the full employment budget surplus, i.e. the deficit or surplus that would occur if the economy were at full employment) did not always possess the correct sign and was of low statistical significance.

(3) The response of nominal income to monetary changes (i.e. the monetary multiplier) was substantial and fast-acting (the main effect occurring within three quarters). The response to fiscal policy declined as time elapsed so that it was practically zero after five quarters.

(4) The proportion of changes in income explained by changes in the money supply and changes in the fiscal variable was within the range 53–73 per cent. This was a particularly high figure bearing in mind that estimation was in the form of first differences and also that the effect of other exogenous variables were excluded from the estimating equation.

Naturally enough, these results which belittled the role of fiscal policy stirred up considerable controversy. In particular, De Leeuw and Kalchbrenner (1969) modified the fiscal variable to allow for fiscal drag (i.e. any automatic change in the full employment budget surplus/deficit) owing to price increases (that for real income changes was already allowed for in the concept of the full employment budget surplus). When they re-estimated the Andersen–Jordan equations they found that the monetary multiplier was still powerful but operated with a longer lag, whereas the coefficient for the fiscal variable became statistically significant implying a multiplier rising to 2.5. Similar tests on UK data have been carried out by Artis and Nobay (1969) and, while not expressing a high degree of confidence in their results, they found a very weak monetary multiplier but a strong fiscal multiplier. However, subsequent estimates on UK data by other researchers have obtained very similar results to those reported by Andersen and Jordan (1968).

The methodology behind single-equation estimates, where income is subject to substantial shocks from variables excluded from the equation estimated, has been heavily criticised (see e.g. Modigliani, 1977). It is argued that, at their best, single-equation estimates are a poor representation of the truth and recourse must then be made to evidence provided by large scale macroeconometric models. In particular, Modigliani and Ando (1976) have reported the results of estimating a reduced-form equation of the type used by Andersen and Jordan (1968) from a synthetic GNP series generated by the MPS model of the US economy. They then examined how far the response of national income to changes in government expenditure, as evidenced by the estimated reduced-form equation, resembled the true response path of the MPS model. In fact the response path inferred from the reduced form equations 'bore no recognisable relation' to the true path within the MPS model. It does not matter for the significance of this simulation exercise whether the MPS model represents the true structure of the economy. The key point is that the reduced-form estimates, from data generated by that model, inferred a time path in response to changes in government expenditure that bore little resemblance to that built into the model that generated the data. They also reported in this study that similar results were obtained when the simulated experiment described above was repeated for three other macroeconomic models of the US economy which varied quite widely in size.

It would appear that the single-equation technique is quite unreliable, and we shall now examine whether reliable empirical evidence can be obtained from simulation experiments on large-scale econometric models.

6.6.2 *Simulation of econometric models*

Various econometric models of the US economy have been constructed and these are invariably labelled according to the bodies who constructed them. In this section we shall refer to models prepared by: the Bureau of Economic Analysis (BEA); the University of Michigan (Michigan); the Federal Reserve Bank of St Louis (St Louis); the University of Wharton (Wharton); the MIT–Penn–Social Science Research Council (MPS). One of the best summaries has been presented by Christ (1975), in which he reviewed the performance of several econometric models of the US economy and their consistency in forecasting the relative importance of fiscal and monetary policy. He concluded that 'they disagree so strongly about the effects of important monetary and fiscal policies, that they cannot be considered reliable guides to such policy effects, until it can be determined which of them are wrong in this respect and which, (if any), are right.' In terms of real GNP, there is a fair amount of agreement for the first two years following the sustained change of policy, with estimates of multipliers for government expenditure (without accommodating monetary policy) ranging between 1.4 and 2.4–with the sole exception of the St Louis model, which puts the five-quarter multiplier (and all subsequent ones) close to zero. However, with simulation beyond two years the agreement vanishes. Three models show negative multipliers indicating there is over-crowding out (—0.5 for the MPS model after twenty quarters; —3 and —23(!) after forty quarters for the Wharton and BEA models respectively). The multiplier for one other model (Michigan) falls to zero after forty quarters and those for four other models fall below their peak value by between 10 and 66 per cent. To confuse the matter even further, the value of the multiplier for one other model surveyed was still rising after forty quarters but started to drop after fifty-six quarters and was still falling at sixty-four quarters!

It is clear that we do not get a precise unambiguous answer as to how potent fiscal policy is in the long run from the simulation exercises of econometric models. Nevertheless, we do get an indication of the length of time involved in the long run (at least twenty quarters) and some evidence supporting the view that crowding out in real terms does occur at least to some extent. Also, apart from the St Louis model, there is no evidence at all of crowding out in nominal terms – even after forty quarters the nominal multipliers range between a low of 2.5 to a high of 5.9 depending on the model concerned.

6.7   Conclusions

What conclusions can be drawn about the potency of fiscal policy? A fairly general consensus seems to be possible in that a sustained fiscal policy can influence real and nominal income in the short run with a peak effect occurring in about two years. Thereafter the effect of fiscal policy on real, but not nominal, income declines, so that in the long run there is very little if any effect on real income; i.e., crowding out occurs. If this is so it is open to both Keynesians and monetarists to claim victory; to Keynesians because fiscal policy is powerful in the short run, and to monetarists because the peak value of the multiplier for real income is considerably smaller than that envisaged in the 1950s and 1960s and also because crowding out seems likely to occur in the long run. The argument so far has been discussed in terms of an increase in government expenditure. Presumably the converse would hold true for reductions in government expenditure. These should be followed in the long run by crowding in of private expenditure, especially investment, leading to a quicker growth in the capacity of economy. This seems to be the economic rationale for the argument put forward by some monetarists that a reduction in government expenditure would lead to a faster rate of growth in the economy in the long run.

However, it is appropriate at this stage to recall the major qualification to the analysis made earlier. Throughout this chapter it has been assumed that the government expenditure is on non-productive services or goods from the private sector; i.e., it is a dead weight on the economy. If however the government expenditure is productive (e.g. investment in the economic infrastructure or nationalised industries), then similar results would accrue to government expenditure as to private investment. Both types of investment would raise the capacity of the economy. We should also like to stress that the discussion of fiscal policy has been directed towards its ability to influence the level of income and not towards its ability to influence income distribution and resource allocation. Discussion of this latter function is dependent on how efficient the market is in performing that function, a discussion that is outside the context of this book.

Bibliography

Titles marked * are particularly recommended for student reading.

Andersen, L. C. and Jordan, J. L. (1968), 'Monetary and Fiscal Actions: a Test of their Relative Importance in Economic Stabilisation'. *Federal Reserve Bank of St Louis Monthly Review* (November).

Artis, M. J. and Nobay, A. R. (1961), 'Two Aspects of the Monetary Debate'. *National Institute Economic Review* (August).

Barro, R. J. (1974), 'Are Government Bonds Net Wealth?' *Journal of Political Economy*, vol. 82 (November/December).

Blinder, A. S. and Solow, R. M. (1973), 'Does Fiscal Policy Matter?' *Journal of Public Economics*, vol. 2.

Blinder, A. S. and Solow, R. M. (1976), 'Does Fiscal Policy Still Matter?' *Journal of Monetary Economics*, vol. 2.

Brunner, K. (1971), 'A Survey of Selected Issues in Monetary Theory'. *Revue Suisse d'Economie Politique et de Statistique*, vol. 107.

Brunner, K. and Meltzer, A. (1976), 'Government, the Private Sector and Crowding Out'. *The Banker*, vol. 126 (July).

*Carlson, K. M. and Spencer, R. W. (1975), 'Crowding Out and Its Critics'. *Reserve Bank of St Louis Monthly Review* (December).

Christ, C. F. (1968), 'A Simple Macroeconomic Model with a Government Budget Restraint.' *Journal of Political Economy*, vol. 76 (January/February).

Christ, C. F. (1975), 'Judging the Performance of Econometric Models of the U.S.A. Economy'. *International Economic Review*, vol. 16 (February).

*Currie, D. A. (1978), 'Macroeconomic Policy and the Government Financing Requirement: A Survey of Recent Developments'. *Forthcoming in 1977 AUTE Conference Proceedings*.

De Leeuw, F. and Kalchbrenner, J. (1969), 'Monetary and Fiscal Actions: A Test of their Relative Importance in Economic Stabilisation: A Comment'. *Federal Reserve Bank of St Louis Monthly Review* (April).

Friedman, M. (1971a), 'Government Revenue from Inflation'. *Journal of Political Economy*, vol. 79 (July/August).

Friedman, M. (1971b), 'A Monetary Theory of Nominal Income'. *Journal of Political Economy*, vol. 79 (March/April).

Friedman, M. (1972), 'Comment on the Critics'. *Journal of Political Economy*, vol. 80 (September/October).

Friedman, M. (1976), 'Comments on Tobin and Buiter'. *Monetarism*, edited by J. L. Stein (Amsterdam: North Holland).

Modigliani, F. (1977), 'The Monetarist Controversy or Should We Forsake Stabilisation Policies?' *American Economic Review*. vol. 67 (March).

Modigliani, F. and Ando, A. (1976), 'Impacts of Fiscal Actions on Aggregate Income and the Monetarist Controversy: Theory and Evidence'. In *Monetarism*, edited by J. L. Stein (Amsterdam: North Holland).

Ott, D. J. and Ott, A. F. (1965), 'Budget Balance and Equilibrium Income'. *Journal of Finance*, vol. 20 (March).

Pesek, B. P. and Saving, T. R. (1967), *Money, Wealth and Economic Theory* (New York: Collier Macmillan).

Radcliffe Committee (1959), Committee on the Working of the Monetary System *Report* Cmnd. 827 (London: HMSO).

7 Money and the Balance of Payments

Our aim in this chapter is to examine the link between money and the balance of payments, but first of all it is desirable to review briefly the main theories of the balance of payments in order to set the various approaches into a historical perspective.

7.1 Review of balance of payments theories

7.1.1 *Exchange rate regimes*

As a first step it is useful to recapitulate the definition of the exchange rate and the distinction between fixed and floating exchange rates set out in chapter 3. The exchange rate is the price of domestic currency in terms of foreign currency. Under fixed exchange rates the price of the domestic currency can be altered only by government decisions to devalue or revalue the currency. In contrast, under floating/flexible exchange rates the market forces of demand and supply will determine the level of the exchange rate. Under clean/pure floating there is no government intervention, whereas with dirty/managed floating the government intervenes to influence the level of the exchange rate. The distinction between the two extremes of fixed and pure floating exchange rates is important for analysing a country's balance of payments position. Under fixed exchange rates it is possible (at least in the short run) for a country to experience balance of payments disequilibria (deficits or surpluses); whereas under a pure floating regime the price of the domestic currency in terms of foreign currency (the exchange rate) will adjust to clear the foreign exchange market. Since with a pure float the level of official reserves will remain constant, the combined balance of the remaining accounts (i.e. current and capital) will be zero.

7.1.2   *The gold standard*

The gold standard was a particular form of a system of fixed exchange rates within which the price of gold was fixed in terms of domestic currency, and therefore the exchange rate was determined for all countries adhering to this standard by the ratios of gold prices specified in domestic currencies. Since the exchange rate was fixed, a balance of payments surplus would be met by inflows of international specie (gold). This approach, known as the price–specie flow mechanism, was especially linked with the work of David Hume. With the domestic money supply based on gold, the inflow of gold induced by a balance of payments surplus would cause in its turn an expansion of the domestic money supply. In line with the traditional quantity theory outlined in chapter 2, it was believed that this would drive up the domestic price level. If the rate of increase of the domestic price level was faster than the rate at which the rest of the world price level was increasing, then imports would expand and exports contract until such time as the balance of payments surplus was eliminated. Conversely, a balance of payments deficit would entail an outflow of gold, which would result in a decrease in the domestic money supply and the domestic price level; and the falling prices would be expected to improve the balance of payments. Thus the important prediction of this approach was that there was an automatic adjustment mechanism which would lead to the correction of balance of payments disequilibria, and it was on the basis of this prediction that David Hume attacked mercantilist policies of accumulating precious metals through balance of payments surpluses. Within this analysis, then, the supply of domestic money is adjusted to the demand for it through balance of payments deficits/surpluses. As we shall see later, the monetary approach to the balance of payments also includes an automatic adjustment mechanism, but one that is based on the link between expenditure and the demand for real balances relative to the supply of money at the ruling price level, rather than the departure of the domestic price level (even if only temporarily) from that ruling in the rest of the world.

7.1.3 *The elasticities approach*

The next main approach, the elasticities approach, was initiated against a background of mass unemployment in the 1930s and the collapse of the international regime of fixed exchange rates. At the same time, the Keynesian revolution transformed the theoretical base of macroeconomic analysis from one of full employment with wages and prices flexible in both directions to one of general unemployment with wages and prices that would not fall in response to excess supply (i.e., they were rigid downwards). These developments led to a basic change in the theoretical approach to balance of payments problems. The balance of payments was no longer seen to adjust automatically, and this led to an examination of how government economic policy could improve the balance of payments and, in particular, the conditions under which devaluation would be successful in doing just this. The alteration of quantities of exports and imports in response to relative price changes was a vital component of this analysis. In order to develop this point further, the relative price of domestic to foreign goods can be defined as:

$$\frac{eP}{P_W}$$

where (1) e = the exchange rate expressing domestic currency in terms of foreign currency (e.g. £ in terms of $: in mid-1977 e = approximately 1.70);

(2) P = the domestic price of goods in terms of domestic currency;

(3) P_W = the world price of goods in terms of foreign currency.

Therefore with fixed prices the relative price of home to foreign goods could be altered only by changing the exchange rate. As a result, this approach stressed the elasticities of home demand for imports and foreign demand for exports, and concentrated on the necessary conditions for the current account of the balance of payments to improve following a devaluation (i.e. a reduction in e). Assuming both an initially balanced trade position and infinite elasticities of supply based on mass unemployment, the necessary condition was that the sum of the elasticities of home and foreign demand for imports should exceed unity (the Marshall–Lerner condition). Relaxing the assumptions does not in fact alter the fundamental basis of the analysis, but merely causes the necessary conditions to become more complicated mathematically. Subsequent developments incorporated the Keynesian multiplier analysis into the model. Since the real home currency value of net exports is a component of aggregate demand, any increase in the real quantity of exports and/or reduction in the real quantity of imports achieved through devaluation would lead to a multiplied expansion in domestic real income. This would arise because, in a situation of mass unemployment, resources would be available to meet the increased demand for output. As aggregate demand increased, so imports would also increase and this would partially offset the initial improvement in the balance of payments. However, with a positive marginal propensity to save and a progressive tax rate system, the final outcome would still be an improvement in the balance of payments.

7.1.4 *The absorption approach*

After the Second World War, with the continuous maintenance of high levels of employment, the elasticities approach became in- adequate in view of its implicit assumption of the availability of unemployed resources to meet the increase in output needed to improve the balance of payments following a successful devaluation. This omission tended to be rectified by the development of the absorption approach with its emphasis on total payments and expenditure (see e.g. Johnson, 1958). In this connection we can define:

$$B \equiv R_f - P_f \tag{7.1}$$

where (1) B = balance of payments;

(2) R_f = receipts from non-residents;

(3) P_f = payments to non-residents.

Receipts from residents equal by definition payments to residents by residents; i.e.,

$$R_r \equiv P_r \tag{7.2}$$

where (1) R_r = receipts from residents;

(2) P_r = payments by residents to residents.

Using (7.2) and (7.1),

$$B \equiv (R_f + R_r) - (P_f + P_r). \tag{7.3}$$

By definition:

$$R \equiv R_f + R_r \tag{7.4}$$

$$P \equiv P_f + P_r \tag{7.5}$$

where (1) R = total receipts by residents;
   (2) P = total payments by residents.

Substituting (7.4) and (7.5) into (7.3),

$$B \equiv R - P. \tag{7.6}$$

The capital account is usually ignored in this analysis, so that

$$B \equiv Y - E \tag{7.7}$$

where (1) B = current account (exports–imports);
   (2) Y = output or GNP;
   (3) E = domestic expenditure or absorption $(C + I + G)$
(all variables in nominal terms).

Since the current account of the balance of payments is equal by definition to output less absorption, a balance of payments deficit will occur when the flow of absorption is greater than the flow of output and conversely a surplus when production is greater than absorption.

The main prediction of this approach can be seen from identity (7.7); that is, in order to improve the balance of payments it is necessary either (1) to reduce absorption (expenditure) relative to output (expenditure-reducing policies), or (2) to increase output relative to absorption (expenditure-switching policies); or (3) possibly to employ some combination of the two alternatives.

The absorption approach recognised that in a situation of full employment devaluation alone would be insufficient for correcting a balance of payments deficit and that a policy of deflation would also be required. Subsequent theoretical analysis, in considering devaluation, showed that one of the channels of achieving improvements in the balance of payments was a reduction in aggregate demand caused by the lowering of the level of real balances (i.e. M/P where M is the nominal quantity of money and P the general price level), consequent upon the rise in the price level following a devaluation. It is worth noting here that this method of adjustment is also stressed in the monetary approach to the balance of payments discussed in section 7.2 below. However, the role of money changes tended to be ignored in the elasticities and absorption approaches with the explicit or sometimes implicit assumption that changes in the money supply, following balance of payments disequilibria, could be sterilised or neutralised by the authorities, so that balance of payments surpluses/deficits could be treated as flow equilibria. In contrast, the monetary approach takes the diametrically opposite view and asserts that, in the long run, changes in the money supply arising out of balance of payments deficits/surpluses cannot be neutralised and that the demand for and supply of money functions are the central theoretical relationships around which analysis of the balance of payments should take place. This does not mean that real (i.e. non monetary) factors do not influence the balance of payments, but rather that their impact should be examined through the effect they have on the demand for and supply of money.

7.2 The monetary approach to the balance of payments (fixed exchange rates)

7.2.1 *Balance of payments: a monetary phenomenon*

In this section we shall discuss the monetary approach to the balance of payments within the context of one extreme exchange rate regime, namely that of fixed exchange rates. For an accessible account of the monetary approach to the balance of payments see Johnson (1972b), Kemp (1975) or Whitman (1975).

The monetary approach concentrates primarily on the money market, in which the relationship between the stock demand for and supply of money is regarded as the main determinant of balance of payments flows. Within this approach the following key assumptions (examined more fully later in this section) are usually made:

(1) Both the demand for and supply of money are stable functions of a limited number of variables.

(2) Long-run equilibrium in a macroeconomic model requires both stock and flow equilibrium in all markets. (This requirement was examined in chapter 6.)

(3) The authorities cannot sterilise balance of payments deficits/ surpluses for any significant period of time.

(4) The approach is concerned almost entirely with the long run, in which output and employment are assumed to tend towards a situation of full employment which is determined mainly by real factors independently of monetary policy.

(5) In the absence of trade barriers, and after allowing for transport costs, perfect commodity arbitrage will ensure that the law of one price must hold for similar traded goods.

Within the monetary approach, the balance of payments is treated as essentially a monetary phenomenon in which emphasis is given to the relationship between the demand for and supply of money. Any discrepancy between actual and desired money balances will result in balance of payments deficits/surpluses, which in turn provide the mechanism whereby the discrepancy is eliminated. It is, however, essential to note that in this analysis deficits and surpluses now refer to the overall net balance on the current and capital accounts, sometimes called the money account of the balance of payments (in the UK statistics, the balance for official financing). Under fixed exchange rates, a balance of payments surplus can be the result of either an excess demand for money by domestic units, or an excess supply of money created abroad. Conversely, a deficit can be the result of either an excess supply of money created by the domestic monetary authority, (i.e. excessive domestic credit expansion) or an excess demand from abroad. Either way, persistent deficits can occur only if the domestic monetary authority allows domestic credit to expand faster than the public wants to expand its money holdings.

7.2.2 *The balance of payments and the domestic money supply*

Before examining the mechanism that eliminates any discrepancy between actual and desired money balances, it is worthwhile restating briefly the relationship that exists between the balance of payments and the domestic money supply under fixed exchange rates (discussed earlier in chapter 3). A balance of payments deficit leads, *ceteris paribus*, to a reduction in a country's foreign exchange reserves, and therefore to a reduction in the monetary base and hence ultimately in the domestic money supply. Conversely, a balance of payments surplus will lead to an expansion in the money supply. Now of course it is true that these results would occur only if the government does not neutralise those monetary effects, but monetarists argue that neutralisation is impossible in the long run. Clearly the level of foreign currency reserves provides a limit to the duration of time a deficit country can finance a deficit and therefore neutralise the monetary effects, but it is not so clear that there are similar pressures on a surplus country which is continually acquiring reserves. In this connection, some monetarists argue that it is irrational for a country to pursue in the long run a policy of achieving continuous balance of payments surpluses since, in reality, it means that a country is willing to trade, without limit, goods (consumption or investment) for foreign balances.

7.2.3   *The adjustment mechanism in the open economy*

If we assume that sterilisation is not possible in the long run, then the next stage in the analysis is to consider the effects on the economy of an increase in the money supply, consequent upon a balance of payments surplus (the argument in respect of a deficit is the exact converse of the arguments presented below). Central to this analysis is the contention (examined in chapter 2) that there exists a stable demand for money function. Thus with the increase in the nominal quantity of money owing to the balance of payments surplus and an unchanged general price level, real balances (M/P) will rise above their equilibrium value. This divergence between actual and desired real balances will lead to a portfolio adjustment process as discussed in chapter 2. Either one of the arguments of the demand for money function must change if the increased real balances are to be held willingly, and/or alternatively the money will be disposed of by purchasing foreign goods and/or foreign securities, thereby reducing the balance of payments surplus. The second alternative is the transmission mechanism stressed in the monetary approach, but adjustment could take place through interest rate changes altering consumption and/or investment flows until full stock equilibrium is established.

It should be emphasised that the critical assumption, with either of the two alternatives discussed above, is the stability of the money demand function. If this function were unstable, for example in the case of the liquidity trap, the extra level of real balances would be accommodated and willingly held with only very minor changes in the rate of interest and no further repercussions on the economy would arise, no automatic adjustment mechanism would result, and the whole monetary approach would be irrelevant to balance of payments theory (Mussa, 1974). However, the empirical evidence (as discussed in chapter 2) suggests that the money demand function is reasonably stable (behaviourally).

The monetary approach therefore considers the effects on stock equilibrium (defined as a situation where all assets are willingly held) of monetary disturbances arising from balance of payments deficits/surpluses, whereas, in contrast, the elasticities and absorption approaches analyse the balance of payments in flow terms. The monetary approach argues that, to be in long-run equilibrium, the money market must be in full stock equilibrium, otherwise the portfolio of assets would be continually changing, thus inducing changes in the flows of expenditure. This long-run equilibrium cannot occur unless the money account of the balance of payments shows a zero balance. Assuming fixed exchange rates, the money account will be in deficit/surplus when the authorities are purchasing/selling their currency with foreign exchange assets to prevent their currency from depreciating/appreciating. This accounts for the importance assigned to the money account of the balance of payments and illustrates that, in contrast with the emphasis placed on the current account by the elasticities and absorption approaches, the monetary approach does not offer any consideration, let alone explanation, of the individual accounts within the balance of payments. Within this approach, analysis of the balance of payments adjustment must be channelled through the effects a non-zero money account will have on the demand for and supply of money functions.

7.2.4 *Concluding remarks*

In conclusion, then, the monetary approach takes the demand for money function as the demand for an asset. Money market disequilibrium (discrepancy between actual and desired real money balances) will cause flow disequilibrium in the balance of payments as people try to get rid of unwanted real money balances through purchase of goods and/or foreign securities. This adjustment process will continue until such time as the source of the disturbance has ceased, in other words when real balances are back to their desired level, so that there is full stock equilibrium again and the money account of the balance of payments has a zero balance.

Having presented the analysis under fixed exchange rates and before proceeding to the predictions of the monetary approach, it is worth noting that in a world of pure floating rates (i.e. one without intervention by the monetary authorities in the foreign exchange market) the money balance will be zero, and that the counterpart to the monetary approach under floating exchange rates is the asset market determination of exchange rates. This is considered in section 7.4 below.

7.3   Predictions of the monetary approach (fixed exchange rates)

7.3.1   *Development of a simple two-country model*

The predictions of the monetary approach can be illustrated using the following two-country model (see Dornbusch, 1973). In this simple model the stock demand for money (L) is a constant fraction (k) of the price level in domestic currency (P) times real income (y) which is exogenously determined. In contrast, the flow demand for money (referred to henceforth as hoarding, H) arises from the gradual adjustment (Π) of actual money balances (M) to their desired stock (L). The money stock (M) is divided between the endogenous level of foreign exchange reserves (R) and the policy variable domestic credit (D). Nominal expenditure (E) is equal to nominal output ($P\,y$) less hoarding (H); and consequently, in long-run equilibrium with zero hoarding, all output is demanded (i.e., abstracting from the analysis of economic growth, there exists full employment, zero balance of payments and zero hoarding or saving in the long-run equilibrium). In the short run, flows of international reserves will result from nominal expenditure not equalling nominal output. For example, in the short run positive hoarding will lead to a balance of payments surplus and a foreign currency inflow, and for a deficit the converse holds. The assumption of one price is incorporated with the home price in domestic currency equalling the world price in foreign currency via the exchange rate (e) expressed as the domestic price of foreign currency (i.e. $1 equals approximately £0.59, when £1 = $1.70).

More formally, the model can be expressed in the following equations with an asterisk indicating the position of the foreign country, the bar exogenous or policy variables and the dot the rate of change of that variable.

$$L = kP\bar{y} \tag{7.8}$$

$$L^* = k^*P^*\bar{y}^* \tag{7.9}$$

$$P = P^*e \quad \text{or} \quad P^* = P/e \tag{7.10}$$

$$M = \bar{D} + R \tag{7.11}$$

$$M^* = \bar{D}^* + R^* \tag{7.12}$$

$$\dot{R} = B = \dot{M} = -e\dot{R}^* = e\dot{M}^* \tag{7.13}$$

$$E = P\bar{y} - H \tag{7.14}$$

$$E^* = P^*\bar{y}^* - H^* \tag{7.15}$$

$$H = \Pi(L - M) = H(P, M) \tag{7.16}$$

$$H^* = \Pi^*(L^* - M^*) = H^*(P^* M^*) \tag{7.17}$$

This model is depicted diagrammatically in figure 7.1 with the domestic price level shown on the vertical axis and domestic hoarding on the horizontal axis. For the foreign country, however, dis-hoarding valued in domestic currency (i.e. $-eH^*$) is shown on the horizontal axis. From equation (7.16) it can be seen that hoarding occurs because of divergence between actual and desired money balances. Therefore as the domestic price level increases, *ceteris paribus*, the value of real balances will fall below their equilibrium level and increased hoarding will take place. Thus with a given money stock, the hoarding function (H in figure 7.1) will be positively sloped with respect to the price level. From equation (7.10) the foreign price level will rise as the domestic price level rises, given the exchange rate e. Therefore, as the domestic price level rises, the real value of foreign money hoardings will fall below their equilibrium level and increased hoarding will take place. Increased hoarding is the same as decreased dis-hoarding, so the foreign dis-hoarding schedule (H^* in figure 7.1) will be negatively sloped, since the rate of dis-hoarding will increase, *ceteris paribus*, as the price level falls. Flow equilibrium (i.e. no desire to alter expenditure) would occur where the two rates are equal when expressed in the same currency.

$$H = -H^*e . \tag{7.18}$$

In this instance equation (7.18) is satisfied at A_2 in figure 7.1 and there is full stock equilibrium with existing stocks of money willingly held in both countries. As noted earlier in this section, both the hoarding and the dis-hoarding schedules assume a constant nominal stock of money, and if the money supply is changed the position of both schedules would alter. An increase in the domestic money

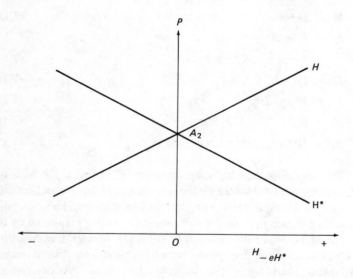

Figure 7.1

supply will cause the hoarding schedule to shift inwards (less hoarding at each price level), and a decrease in the domestic money supply will cause the hoarding schedule to shift outwards. Because negative hoarding is the exact opposite to hoarding, the converse shifts in the dis-hoarding schedule would occur, i.e. inwards in response to a decrease in the foreign money supply and outwards following an increase in the foreign money supply.

We shall use this model in the following sections to demonstrate the predictions of the monetary approach to the balance of payments under conditions of fixed exchange rates.

7.3.2 *Automatic adjustment*

The monetary approach predicts that there is an automatic adjustment mechanism that will operate, without government discretionary policy, to correct balance of payments disequilibria. This adjustment process, as we have seen, operates through balance of payments flows eliminating any disparity between actual and desired real money holdings. Reference to figure 7.1 will show that, if the intersection of schedules H and H^* had been to the left of OP, then this would have implied negative hoarding in the domestic country and negative dis-hoarding (i.e. positive hoarding) in the foreign country. Negative hoarding entails a balance of payments deficit, since reference to equation (7.14) shows that expenditure is greater than output and this will lead to a contraction in the domestic money supply, thus reducing real balances at the initial price level and therefore causing an increase in planned hoarding. The converse is true for the foreign country, where real balances at the initial price level will increase and therefore dis-hoarding will also increase. Both curves would then shift to the right until full stock equilibrium was reached with zero hoarding in both countries; i.e., the intersection would be on the OP line. On the other hand, if intersection was to the right of OP this would have implied positive hoarding in the domestic country and positive dis-hoarding (negative hoarding) in the foreign country, and the adjustment process would have been the opposite to that just discussed; i.e., both the hoarding and dis-hoarding schedules would shift to the left. Thus full equilibrium in the long run is possible only with zero hoarding in both countries, and the resulting equilibrium determines both price levels (given the exchange rate) together with the distribution of world nominal quantity of money between the two countries. This illustrates the prediction of automatic adjustment in the balance of payments since the system will always adjust to full stock equilibrium in the long run, i.e. position A_2 in figure 7.1, with zero balance of payments.

7.3.3   *Power of expenditure-switching policies*

Closely linked to the monetarist view of the existence of a mechanism that ensures the automatic adjustment of balance of payments disequilibria is the prediction that, by themselves, expenditure-switching policies will fail to produce any lasting improvement in the balance of payments. In this context devaluation would raise the domestic price level and hence lower the level of real balances below their equilibrium level, causing domestic residents to attempt to restore their real balances through international commodity and security markets. Hence absorption would be reduced until such time as real balances had been built up to their desired level again, but once equilibrium had been re-established absorption would revert to its previous level and the balance of payments surplus would be eliminated. However, while it is true that no permanent improvement in the balance of payments would occur, the level of foreign currency reserves would increase owing to the temporary surplus, though the transitory beneficial effect on reserves and on the balance of payments could be offset by an increase in the rate of domestic credit expansion. The monetary approach also implies that import quotas, tariffs, exchange controls and other restrictions on trade and payments will improve the balance of payments only if they induce an increase in the demand for money by raising domestic prices. However, like devaluation, the effects will be transitory and will continue only until the stock of money is increased through balance of payments surpluses to meet the increased demand.

This prediction regarding devaluation is examined in figure 7.2. Full stock equilibrium occurs initially at price level P_0. Devaluation can be represented by an upward shift of H^* since for the foreign price level (P/e) to remain constant, and therefore foreign monetary equilibrium to be maintained, the domestic price level would have to rise by the same percentage as the devaluation. Thus H^* shifts upwards to H^{I*}. In line with previous discussion, Q cannot be a long-run equilibrium since hoarding is not zero, and both curves would then shift inwards, with the final price level lying between P_0 and P_1. In the limiting case of a small domestic country relative to the rest of the world, the domestic price would rise to P_1 with no change in the foreign price level. However, it is sometimes argued that expenditure-switching policies are taken at a time when balance of payments disequilibrium exists (i.e. a short-run disequilibrium situation), not from a position of zero balance (i.e. a long-run equilibrium). Therefore, even if it is accepted that no permanent balance of payments surplus would be obtained, such policies could be desirable because they would speed up the adjustment towards equilibrium rather than relying on the allegedly slower automatic adjustment process. The monetarist response to this argument is that, at present, we have insufficient knowledge of how the economy works to carry out such discretionary policies (see chapter 5 for a discussion of the issue of discretionary policies).

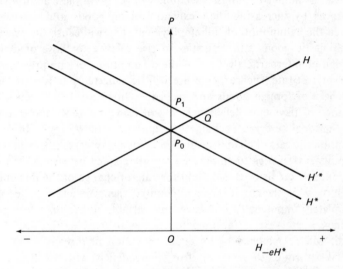

Figure 7.2

7.3.4 *The power of monetary policy*

The last prediction of the monetary approach that we shall examine concerns the power of monetary policy. In the case of a small country maintaining a fixed exchange rate with the rest of the world it is usually assumed, in monetary models, that the country's price level is pegged to the world price level and its interest rate is the world interest rate. In this situation the country's money supply becomes an endogenous rather than a policy variable. The country's money supply consists of its stock of foreign exchange reserves (R)

and the stock of domestic credit (D); i.e.,

$$M_s = R + D .\tag{7.19}$$

Domestic monetary policy will not determine the country's money supply but will only determine the division between foreign exchange reserves and domestic credit. Monetary policy controls the volume of domestic credit (the money supply being endogenous), which in turn influences the balance of payments and hence the foreign exchange reserves of the country. If the domestic monetary authority allows domestic credit to expand faster than the public wants to expand its money holdings, the public will get rid of these additional balances by increasing their expenditure on goods and services. Given the assumption of full employment, this will cause the prices of domestic goods and securities to rise relative to those of their foreign counterparts. Because of the assumptions of one price and one interest rate, such expenditure will be deflected purely into the purchase of foreign goods and securities. In turn this will cause a balance of payments deficit, which will lead to a reduction in the international reserves backing the domestic money supply. In this situation the rate of change of foreign exchange reserves (the balance of payments) varies to eliminate any discrepancy between the rate of domestic credit expansion and the rate of change of the demand for money. In the case of a small country, then, monetary policy is completely impotent to influence any variable (other than foreign exchange reserves) in the long run, since an increase in domestic credit will be matched by an equal reduction in foreign currency reserves (through the balance of payments deficit) with no effect on the money supply. In the absence of the small-country assumption, monetary policy will have some effect depending upon a country's size relative to the rest of the world. The larger the proportionate size of the country, the greater will be the effect of domestic monetary policy; this is particularly relevant to the United States, whose size and importance in the world economy (apart from its reserve currency country status considered later) provides some scope for monetary policy to be effective.

With respect to the prediction concerning the power of monetary policy, we can see from equations (7.11) and (7.16) that, if domestic credit is expanded, negative hoarding would take place as attempts are made to get rid of unwanted money balances. This could be achieved by an outflow of money owing to lower rates of interest, leading to increased foreign lending (i.e. capital outflow) and/or owing to greater spending on imports (i.e. the current account). Referring to figure 7.3, the planned domestic hoarding schedule would shift to the left from H to H^1; in accordance with the adjustment mechanism discussed above point O^1 cannot be a long-run equilibrium and both curves would then shift to the right; and the final equilibrium would lie between A_1 and A_2 with both price levels having increased in response to the increase in world money stock.

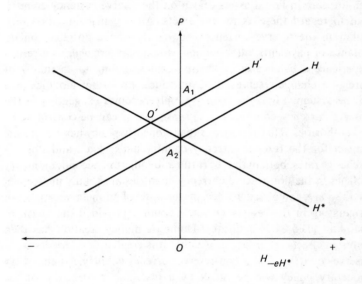

Figure 7.3

In the limiting case of the small country relative to the rest of the world, the effect on world prices would be insignificant and equilibrium would be restored at A_2 in figure 7.3, and with the overall balance of payments again zero foreign currency reserves would have fallen during the period of the deficit. Thus, with nominal money stock constant and lower foreign currency reserves, the net result would be an increase in domestic credit expansion matched by a reduction in reserves but with no change in the quantity of money; in other words, monetary policy would be impotent in the long run.

7.3.5 *Special position of the reserve country*

So far we have assumed that all countries are alike, but in fact the existence of reserve currency countries (those countries whose currency can be used as a reserve asset – i.e. as a substitute for gold – specifically the United States) introduces an asymmetry into the system (Whitman, 1975). The feedback from the reserve currency country's balance of payments to its money supply is effectively broken since the other countries may be willing, up to a point, to acquire certain liquid assets drawn on the reserve currency country and to regard these as reserve assets. An expansionary monetary policy in the reserve currency country may have no effect on its balance of payments, although its trading partners will, as a result, experience a balance of payments surplus leading to an inflow of foreign exchange reserves. This introduces important modifications to the system. First, the money supply becomes exogenous in the reserve currency country, in the sense that it can be controlled by the authorities. This also means that monetary policy has a domestic impact for the reserve currency country under fixed and floating exchange rates, both in the short run and long run. Second, monetary policies in the non-reserve currency countries are totally ineffective, as they are compelled to accept the rate of monetary expansion originating in the reserve currency country provided they wish to maintain fixed exchange rates. Domestic money creation has then different effects according to whether it is created in reserve or non-reserve countries. For a non-reserve currency country, expansionary monetary policy will be offset by a matching contraction of the foreign exchange reserves component of its money supply, whereas money loss by the reserve currency country is low-powered money, but becomes high powered in non-reserve currency countries.

7.3.6 *Concluding remarks*

This concludes the discussion of the predictions of the monetary approach to the balance of payments under fixed exchange rates, but it is again worth stressing the role played in the analysis by the assumption of the stability of the money demand and supply functions. The core of the analysis is that balance of payments deficits/surpluses will lead to predictable changes in the money supply and that, if desired real money balances do not equal the supply of such balances, then adjustment will proceed via the balance of payments until equilibrium is established.

7.4   The monetary approach and floating exchange rates

7.4.1   *Pure floating exchange rates*

The discussion so far has centred on a regime of fixed exchange rates, and the question to be considered now is the relevance of the monetary approach to the other extreme of the exchange rate spectrum, namely a system of pure floating exchange rates. In this context the first point to note is that the money balance in the balance of payments is always zero, since the market clearing mechanism (i.e. variation in the exchange rate) will ensure that the demand for and supply of foreign currency are always equal. Therefore, in the absence of balance of payments surpluses/deficits, the only source of monetary expansion is domestic credit expansion, which is in principle controllable by the government.* This contrasts with the position under fixed exchange rates where the money supply is endogenous. So in a mathematical sense, the model is solved for the exchange rate instead of the money supply as under fixed exchange rates and 'the proximate determinants of exchange rates . . . are the demands for and supplies of various national monies' (Mussa, 1976).

How do these changes affect the predictions of the monetary approach? If the money supply is increased through an expansion of domestic credit, this would lead to a proportionate increase in the domestic price level in the long run owing to the divergence arising between the supply of and demand for money in the context of an exogenously determined real income. In its turn, the rise in the domestic price level will, given the law of one price, bring about an exactly equivalent depreciation of the exchange rate in the long run. More formally, referring to equation (7.10), if,

$$P = eP^* \tag{7.10}$$

* This is true as a statement of general principle. However, in the context of the actual money stock definitions found in practice, the quantity of money is sometimes influenced by the state of the balance of payments even in a regime of pure floating exchange rates. For a discussion of the relationship between the UK M_3 definition of money and the balance of payments, see the *Midland Bank Review*, Autumn 1977.

then a 10 per cent increase in P must be matched by a 10 per cent increase in e (i.e. a 10 per cent depreciation, remembering that e is the domestic price of foreign currency). Following this line of reasoning, it is evident that the direction of causation runs from domestic credit expansion through domestic price changes to exchange rate changes rather than initiating from exchange rate changes.

In more complicated models, allowing for variations in real income and also changes in foreign prices in response to world monetary changes, the monetary approach predicts that the rate of change of the exchange rate will depend on the relative rates of monetary expansion and growth of real income in the domestic country compared with those in the rest of the world. If, for example, the net rate of monetary expansion in the domestic country is less than that in the rest of the world, the exchange rate will appreciate; in the converse case it will depreciate. It is also worth recalling from chapter 4 that changes in the world price level will have no effect on domestic prices in the long run, since they will produce an exactly offsetting change in the exchange rate to maintain the equality between P and P^*, provided expectations of future inflation rates are formed with respect to domestic variables only.

Similarly, in the short run, the demand for and supply of the various national currencies will determine the exchange rate, but in this case deviations, albeit temporary ones, are permitted from the law of one price. However, despite the similarities of the requirement for stock equilibrium in the money market, the adjustment to equilibrium is different under fixed exchange rates from that under floating exchange rates. Under the former exchange rate system, the quantity of money adjusts to the real quantity demanded through the balance of payments flows, whereas under pure floating exchange rates it is changes in the price level and exchange rates that, with a constant nominal stock of money, bring about changes in the value of this stock until the real quantity of money demanded equals the nominal quantity supplied at the ruling price level.

7.4.2   *Managed floating exchange rates*

So far we have discussed the monetary approach in the context of fixed and pure floating exchange rate systems. Under a fixed exchange rate system monetary policy will directly influence the country's balance of payments position, whereas under a pure floating regime it will help to determine the exchange rate. However, under a system of managed floating it is usually implicitly assumed that a situation somewhere between the fixed and pure floating rate situations will prevail, with monetary policy influencing both a country's balance of payments position and its exchange rate. If there is fairly heavy intervention by the authorities to manage the exchange rate, then the position will be a fairly close approximation to that prevailing in the case of fixed exchange rates (i.e., the predictions of the analysis will be very similar to those discussed in sections 7.3.2 – 7.3.4). This is true whether or not the government enters into a formal commitment to maintain the exchange rate at any specified level. On the other hand, if government intervention is limited to smoothing out day-to-day fluctuations in the exchange rate without influencing trend movements, official purchases and sales of foreign currency will be roughly equal over any time period other than the very short run. In this case, with official reserves remaining constant, the position will closely approximate that under pure floating exchange rates. What matters then, in the context of a managed float, is the degree of government intervention.

7.4.3 *Concluding remarks*

Finally in this section, it is interesting to note that this view of exchange rate determination is of course quite different from the traditional view of the role of the current account providing flows of foreign currency on to the market, which, when supplemented by largely independent capital flows, determine the exchange rate. We now wish to consider the various criticisms that have been offered against the monetary approach and its predictions.

7.5 Criticisms of the monetary approach

7.5.1 *Law of one price*

It is apparent that the law of one price, which asserts that, in a world of highly integrated markets, a single price must prevail for similar goods and securities, is of dubious validity, especially in the short run. It is certainly true that the law of one price is a feature of many models of the monetary approach to the balance of payments (e.g. the example used in this chapter); but monetarists argue that this assumption is used only as a simplification to facilitate the exposition of the model and is not essential to the analysis. What is essential is that, after due allowances for tariffs and transport costs, prices of identical traded goods will be equalised in the long run. Temporary departures are permissable, but in the long run arbitrage would ensure equality. Existence of traded and non-traded goods will complicate the exposition of the analysis, but will not invalidate the results.

7.5.2   *Neutralisation*

The most important potential source of criticism is whether governments other than in the reserve currency country can and do neutralise the monetary impact of balance of payments surpluses/deficits on the domestic money supply. Referring back to the government budget constraint introduced in chapter 3, it will be recalled that

$$\Delta H \equiv PSD - OMO - NMD - BP \qquad (7.20)$$

where   (1) ΔH = changes in high powered money;
           (2) PSD = public sector deficit;
           (3) OMO = net open market operations;
           (4) NMD = non-marketable debt;
           (5) BP = finance arising through balance of payments deficits.

In principle neutralisation (i.e. offsetting the change in BP so that ΔH remains constant at zero) can occur either through: (1) open market operations by the central bank (i.e. offsetting increases in OMO or NMD) or (2) unbalanced government budgets (offsetting increases in PSD). In the short or medium term a country may be able to maintain a balance of payments surplus by sterilisation operations involving offsetting sales of domestic securities in the home market. It is readily apparent, however, that neutralisation cannot be achieved over the long run through open market operations, since this would require (on the assumption of a balanced government budget) an equal private sector surplus which the general public was willing to allocate entirely (and without limit!) to the required sales of government debt, either directly or indirectly via financial intermediaries. This would clearly violate any reasonable assumptions concerning the portfolio choice of assets; while in the case of a balance of payments deficit, the reduction in the country's holdings of foreign exchange reserves will limit any maintenance of the deficit in the long term.

On the other hand, the incorporation of the government budget constraint (7.20) does reveal another avenue through which neutralisation can occur. Suppose there was a balance of payments surplus and the government chose to run an equivalent budget surplus so that the inflow of money from the foreign sector was exactly matched by the outflow of money from the private sector to the government ($PSD=BP$ in 7.20); then there would be no change in ΔH and, therefore, no disturbance of the actual stock of wealth and hence no effect on the flow of expenditure. This has been called a kind of quasi-equilibrium; quasi in the sense of a situation that cannot continue indefinitely. This is certainly true for a deficit country whose holdings of foreign exchange reserves provide a limit to the duration of time for which a balance of payments deficit can be tolerated. Empirical evidence on neutralisation showing a range of experience is far from clear and suggests that some countries have been able to sterilise, at least partially, the effects of the balance of payments on the domestic money supply. In contrast, it would appear that other countries have not been able to neutralise these effects. Nevertheless, this does mean that a government may be able to run balance of payments surpluses or deficits for quite long periods without the automatic adjustment mechanism working; in other words, adjustment becomes discretionary for quite long periods of time.

7.5.3 *The assumption of full employment*

Also in a Keynesian world of unemployment with rigid prices, expenditure-switching policies can have some permanent effect (Currie 1976). Consider a situation where there is a balance of payments deficit matched by a budget deficit, so that there are no forces leading to a contraction in the money supply, and therefore full stock equilibrium exists. A devaluation (assuming correct elasticities) will improve the balance of payments and at the same time increase domestic income, thereby increasing government tax receipts. Thus we have a new full stock equilibrium, with a lower balance of payments deficit matched by a lower government budget deficit; in fact, both could well have been transformed into a surplus. Likewise, a tariff on imports will also raise income and lower the government budget deficit at the same time as improving the balance of payments. In both these instances equality between the balance of payments deficit and government budget deficit will be established at a lower level of deficit, and therefore a permanent improvement in the balance of payments will be obtained. These criticisms would be refuted by the monetarists on the grounds that their analysis is a long-run analysis and should, therefore, correctly assume that a tendency towards full employment is the general rule and that consideration of the Keynesian underemployment fixed-price model is irrelevant, as this situation is only a temporary aberration from the general position of full employment. So again we return to the importance in monetarist analysis of the stability of the economy discussed in chapter 1.

7.5.4 *Time span*

The final point to be considered in this section is the question of length involved in the concept of the long run. The criticism has been made that the monetary approach with its concentration on the long run renders the analysis useless in so far as policy measures towards the balance of payments are determined in a short-run environment. If the long run refers to decades, then, while the analysis may be logically correct, it is clearly irrelevant for policy-makers; on the other hand, if the time span is in the region of, say, five years, then policy-makers need to take into consideration these long-run effects when devising their policy, even though they are mainly concerned with short-run strategy. Most protagonists of this approach tend to think of the shorter rather than the longer time period as being relevant.

7.6 Conclusions

In order to place the various approaches to the balance of payments in their correct perspective, it is useful to view in quite general terms the elasticities approach as an analysis of the direction and magnitude of the impact effects of a devaluation on the balance of trade, whereas the absorption approach examines the response of the economy to these changes (Branson, 1975). Similarly, the contribution of the monetary approach is to demonstrate that long-run equilibrium requires either zero balance in the money account of the balance of payments or, alternatively, neutralisation of the effects of a non-zero balance of payments on the domestic money supply. Apart from remedying the general failure to consider adequately the role of money in balance of payments theory, the monetary approach also demonstrates that the domestic money supply becomes an endogenous, rather than a policy, variable under fixed exchange rates.

While it is too simplistic and undesirable in practice to categorise economists into rigid schools, some insight into the wide range of views encompassed by the monetary approach to the balance of payments may be obtained by distinguishing between the soft and hard versions of this approach. The soft version (e.g. Fand, 1975) is in accord with the above comments and also stresses that the effects of balance of payments policies can be examined only within the context of a complete macroeconomic model (including the monetary sector) of the economy, and that partial equilibrium analysis can, and often does, give misleading results. Hence the ultimate effect of devaluation can be analysed only in conjunction with the other policies being followed at that time. In addition, the importance attached to asset market determination of exchange rates in a world of floating exchange rates has, once expectations are taken into consideration, provided insight into why exchange rates can vary independently of the state of the current account balance and also into why short-term fluctuations in the rate might be expected (e.g. owing to shifts in portfolio preferences). The soft version also recognises the limited advantage of floating exchange rates in that an independent monetary policy can be pursued because the link between the domestic money supply and the balance of payments is severed, and therefore the country is able, in the long run, to choose its own rate of inflation, with changes in the exchange rate taking up any divergence between this rate and that ruling in the rest of the world. On the other hand, adoption of floating rates does not completely insulate the economy from the rest of the world, in particular from monetary or real disturbances. For example, if there is increased foreign demand for a country's securities, then the exchange rate will appreciate and the trade balance worsen, leading to a rise in unemployment.

In contrast, the hard version, or global monetarism as it is sometimes called, stresses additionally the growing interdependence of the individual economies in the world and argues therefore that analysis must be on the basis of a single world economy rather than individual national units. It is maintained that this growing interdependence has led to near perfect substitutability and arbitrage across national boundaries in both commodity and asset markets. Furthermore, the monetary effects of balance of payments deficits and surpluses cannot, it is argued, be neutralised other than in the very short term, and therefore expenditure-switching policies are impotent to secure improvement of the balance of payments other than in the short run. In any case, it is argued that such policies are irrelevant in view of the automatic corrective mechanism which would eliminate deficits fairly quickly making the transition period unimportant. Thus, by similar reasoning, not only are floating rates unnecessary, but fixed exchange rates have the added advantage that they promote efficiency in world trade. Hence global monetarists, in contrast with other monetarists, advocate fixed exchange rates.

Bibliography

*Titles marked * are particularly recommended for student reading.*

Branson, W. H. (1975), discussion of Whitman (1975), *Brookings Papers on Economic Activity*, no. 3.

Currie, D. A. (1976), 'Some Criticisms of the Monetary Analysis of Balance of Payments Correction'. *Economic Journal*, vol. 86 (September).

Dornbusch, R. (1973), 'Devaluation, Money and Nontraded Goods'. *American Economic Review*, vol. 63 (December).

Fand, D. I. (1975), discussion of Whitman (1975), *Brookings Papers on Economic Activity*, no. 3.

Johnson, H. G. (1958), 'Towards a General Theory of the Balance of Payments', chapter 6 in his *International Trade and Economic Growth: Studies in Pure Theory* (London: Allen & Unwin).

Johnson, H. G. (1972a), 'The Monetary Approach to the Balance of Payments' in his *Further Essays in Monetary Economics* (London: Allen & Unwin).

* Johnson, H. G. (1972b), *Inflation and the Monetarist Controversy*, chapter 3. (Amsterdam: North Holland.)

* Johnson, H. G. (1977), 'The Monetary Approach to the Balance of Payments: A Nontechnical Guide'. *Journal of International Economics*, vol. 7 (August).

* Kemp, D. S. (1975), 'A Monetary View of the Balance of Payments'. *Federal Reserve Bank of St Louis Review*, vol. 57 (April).

Mussa, M. (1974), 'A Monetary Approach to Balance of Payments Analysis'. *Journal of Money Credit and Banking*, vol. 6 (August).

Mussa, M. (1976), 'The Exchange Rate, The Balance of Payments and Monetary and Fiscal Policy under a Regime of Controlled Floating'. *Scandinavian Journal of Economics*, vol. 78.

* Whitman, M. V. N. (1975), 'Global Monetarism and the Monetary Approach to the Balance of Payments'. *Brookings Papers on Economic Activity*, no. 3.

8 Conclusion

From the discussion of the preceding chapters it should be apparent that monetarism is first and foremost a policy-orientated doctrine, founded on both empirical and theoretical bases. The various policy prescriptions that follow from the doctrine are themselves closely interrelated to form a coherent package designed to create a more stable economic environment than has existed since 1945.

During the 1950s through to the mid-1960s, instability in Western capitalist economies was largely reflected in the problem of inflation. From the end of the 1960s many economies have experienced not only high rates of inflation but also high levels of unemployment. The policy prescriptions advocated by monetarists are essentially long-term policies. They are primarily designed to avoid, rather than to cure, the instability that monetarists argue has resulted from the adoption of incorrect policy measures. Nevertheless, monetarists do suggest how macroeconomic policy should be conducted within the transition period when control over monetary expansion is being established. In essence, they suggest an approach whereby the actual rate of monetary expansion is gradually reduced to the desired rate. Such an approach would reduce the social and political cost of the high unemployment that would result from a rapid reduction in the rate of monetary expansion. In addition, they envisage the use of such measures as indexation to assist the transition to the attainment of the specified rate of monetary expansion.

Although the policy prescriptions form an interrelated framework, it is possible for individual policy measures to be judged favourably by both Keynesians and monetarists. Also, in a number of theoretical areas (e.g. the transmission mechanism), the difference between the so-called Keynesian and monetarist schools of thought is one of degree rather than of principle. As a result the polarised split of economists into two quite separate schools is both undesirable and too simplistic. Many of the divisive issues between monetarists and Keynesians can be reduced to a set of empirically testable propositions, and as more empirical evidence becomes available it should be possible to settle certain areas of controversy. However, a word of caution is appropriate here. The question of the validity of the tests used, and therefore of the resulting conclusions, will still remain. For example, we discussed in chapter 1 the Keynesian preference for large-scale detailed econometric models as opposed to the monetarist preference for small-scale models of the economy.

8.1   Monetarists and Keynesians: The Main Differences

There would appear to be two main differences between Keynesian and monetarist schools of thought. First, there is disagreement over the source of the main disturbances that affect the economy. Second, there exists the controversial question of whether there is a long-run trade-off between inflation and unemployment. These differences, in turn, have implications for the policy measures advocated by Keynesians and monetarists.

8.1.1   *The monetarist view*

Monetarists believe that most of the disturbances that affect the economy are monetary in origin. This belief in the predominance of monetary impulses is, as we have discussed, embodied within both the traditional and the modern quantity theory approaches. They also contend that, unless disturbed by erratic monetary growth, the economies of developed countries are inherently stable at a generally acceptable level of unemployment. In consequence, monetarists argue that the rate of growth of the money supply should be controlled and that the authorities should follow a monetary rule. It is feared that discretionary policy could turn out to be destabilising owing to the length and variability of the time lag between monetary changes and their effects on economic activity. Regarding fiscal policy, monetarists have been critical of the way in which Keynesian analysis has tended to neglect the interdependence between monetary and fiscal policy (i.e. the government budget constraint and the way in which a budget deficit is financed). Indeed, it is contended that

fiscal policy actions by themselves are largely ineffective in influencing the level of economic activity. Owing to these beliefs, monetarists
argue that fiscal policy should be replaced by monetary policy as
the main tool of economic stabilisation. The main role of fiscal
policy would then be to influence income distribution and resource
allocation.

Monetarists also believe that there is no trade-off between inflation
and unemployment in the long run. The belief that the long-run
Phillips curve is vertical implies that any attempt by the government
to maintain unemployment below the natural rate will result in an
accelerating rate of inflation.

Because it is believed that policy-makers lack precise knowledge
of the level of the natural rate of unemployment, the analysis
implies that the government should not attempt to aim at a target
unemployment rate. If governments wish to reduce the natural rate
of unemployment in order to achieve higher employment levels,
monetarist analysis suggests that they should pursue microeconomic
policies rather than macroeconomic policies. Such policies could be
directed towards improving the structure of the labour market in the
provision of both (a) information concerning vacancies and (b) the
incentives and opportunities for individuals to acquire the skills
necessary to fill those vacancies in the expanding sectors of the
economy. Thus, by stimulating both the geographical and occupa-
tional mobility of labour, a significant reduction in the level of the
natural rate of unemployment could be obtained (see e.g. Laidler,
1972). Additional measures could be directed towards increasing the
efficiency of industry (e.g. policies directed towards the structure of
industry) so that, in the long run, the demand for labour would
increase.

Using a similar analysis to that discussed for unemployment,
monetarists also contend that monetary policy cannot be used to peg
the rate of interest for other than limited periods of time. If the
authorities increase the rate of monetary expansion in order to
lower the rate of interest, monetarists believe that it will lead to a
rise in the rate of inflation. This would eventually cause the nominal
rate of interest to rise so that equilibrium would be re-established at
the same real rate of interest but at a higher nominal rate. The
implication of monetarist analysis is that, if the government wishes
to reduce the nominal rate of interest, policies should be directed to
(a) reducing the rate of inflation and (b) improving the structure of
financial markets.

It should be emphasised that monetarist analysis does not automatically imply a policy of non-intervention. What is implied is that no permanent reduction can be obtained through monetary expansion in either the level of unemployment or the rate of interest. The appropriate intervention should be micro-based and should be aimed directly at the sector in which the authorities desire improvement.

8.1.2 *The Keynesian view*

In contrast to the monetarist views discussed above, Keynesians argue that most of the disturbances that affect the economy occur from the real sector. In addition, they contend that the economy can settle at a position where unemployment remains at an unacceptably high level for long periods of time. Keynesians advocate the use of discretionary fiscal policy to offset the fluctuations in the level of economic activity, which are held to be due mainly to real disturbances. Such policies are considered necessary to maintain the economy at a high and stable level of employment. Discretionary fiscal policy is prescribed as the effects of fiscal policy changes are considered to be both more predictable and faster acting on economic activity than those of discretionary monetary policy.

Most Keynesians also believe that there is a trade-off between inflation and unemployment in the long run. It is argued that the government can and should pursue an unemployment target via discretionary demand-management policies. Such policies will, however, involve inflation owing to the trade-off between unemployment and inflation. Keynesians believe that the long-run Phillips curve can be shifted downwards (i.e. achieving a lower rate of inflation at any given level of unemployment) by, for example, the adoption of prices and incomes policies. It is possible, however, for a Keynesian to accept the view that, in the long run, there is no trade-off and still maintain that real disturbances (e.g. changes in the marginal efficiency of investment) are more important than monetary disturbances in explaining short-run fluctuations in income.

8.1.3 *Additional remarks*

Goodhart (1975) has pointed out that the attraction of relinquishing discretionary policies in favour of a monetary rule is dependent on three propositions. These are (1) that the demand for money is relatively stable, (2) that there is a unique natural rate of unemployment and (3) that the real economy is basically stable. As we have discussed earlier, in chapters 2, 4 and 1 respectively, all three propositions are contentious. Goodhart has also pointed out that, if the economy takes some time to return to its equilibrium level, the authorities will be under considerable political pressure to accelerate the recovery when unemployment is high. Acceptance by the authorities that policies should be directed towards the long term also requires that the general public should be convinced of this.

8.2 Monetarism and a political stance

Finally, it is worth considering the association of monetarism with right-wing political views. We will not attempt to define so-called left- and right-wing views, as this is a problematic area in itself and is, in any case, irrelevant to the discussion that follows. In Britain this alleged association has largely been fostered through the media which have not been slow to highlight the fact that such controversial political figures as Enoch Powell and Sir Keith Joseph have advocated monetarist policy measures. It has also resulted from the failure of the media to distinguish between Friedman's personal political opinions on certain topics and his contribution to economic analysis.

The view that the proximate cause of inflation is due to monetary expansion put forward by monetarists is, for example, compatible with a wide range of political views. It is possible to be a Marxist and accept the monetarist explanation of inflation. For example, Cobham (1974) has presented a Marxist explanation of inflation along the monetarist lines that the acceleration of inflation in the late 1960s was a consequence of the financing of the Vietnam War via monetary expansion by the United States. Under the system of fixed exchange rates that existed up to 1972–73, the inflationary pressure initiated in America was transmitted to other Western economies through the balance of payments deficit of the United States. The Marxist element in the analysis comes in asking and answering the question of why the Vietnam War was financed in this manner.

The association of monetarism with right-wing political views has led to certain monetarist policy prescriptions being rejected for reasons other than the theoretical and economic rationale underlying them. The dislike of government intervention in macroeconomic policies involving the management of aggregate demand follows automatically from the interrelated aspects of monetarism, rather than from a political stance against government intervention. The belief in the quantity theory, the natural rate hypothesis, the inherent stability of the economy, the irrelevance of allocative detail and the analysis of crowding out, together and individually imply that counter-cyclical fiscal policy has no major role to play in stabilising the economy. In addition, the prescription to follow a monetary rule in order to create a more stable economic environment eliminates the need for discretionary policy. As was pointed out earlier in this chapter, intervention on a micro-basis is quite compatible with monetarist analysis.

In conclusion, despite contrary assertions, it is possible to lean to the left politically and at the same time to (a) accept certain monetarist propositions and (b) advocate the use of fiscal policy to change the distribution of income and allocation of resources. Ironically, these traditional roles assigned to fiscal policy were usurped by the Keynesian revolution. It is possible to be a monetarist without possessing right-wing political leanings and similarly to be a right-wing politician without being a monetarist.

Bibliography

Titles marked * are particularly recommended for student reading.

*Cobham, D. (1974), 'Inflation and Inter-Imperialist Rivalries'. *Marxism Today* (July).
*Cobham, D. (1978), 'The Politics of the Economics of Inflation'. *Lloyds Bank Review* (April).
Goodhart, C. A. E. (1975), *Money, Information and Uncertainty* (London: Macmillan).
Laidler, D. E. W. (1972), 'The Current Inflation – Explanations and Policies'. *National Westminster Bank Quarterly Review* (November).
*Mayer, T. (1975), 'The Structure of Monetarism'. *Kredit und Kapital*, vol. 8.
Meltzer, A. (1977), 'Monetarist, Keynesian and Quantity Theories'. *Kredit und Kapital*, vol. 10.
*Modigliani, F. (1977), 'The Monetarist Controversy or, Should We Forsake Stabilization Policies?' *American Economic Review*, vol. 67 (March).

Index

197